FOUR FUNERALS AND A WEDDING

FOUR FUNERALS AND A WEDDING

A Book About Life, The Universe and a Small French Village

Ben Moss

JANUS PUBLISHING COMPANY
London, England

First published in Great Britain 2009
by Janus Publishing Company Ltd,
105-107 Gloucester Place,
London W1U 6BY

www.januspublishing.co.uk

British Library Cataloguing-in-Publication Data
A catalogue record for this book is available from the British Library

ISBN 978-1-85756-629-1

Cover Design: Janus Publishing
Cover image supplied by Ben Moss

Cover image: 'Gréolières' by Martin Laurance

Printed and bound in Great Britain

For all the Children

The morning wind spreads its fresh smell.
We must get up and take that in,
that wind that lets us live.
Breathe before it's gone.

Jelaluddin Rumi
1207–1273

This is a true story.

However, names of individuals and corporate bodies have been changed where necessary in order to protect their interests, the author's intention being simply to record the events as they occurred.

Chapter 1

June the twenty-ninth, 2003. A damp and gloomy evening in a sombre, late-Victorian terraced house, Norwich, England. And the eve of a major hearing in the High Court, London, the result of which was almost certainly going to save us from what had become, in just eight short weeks since departing for a new life on the French Riviera, a terrifying maelstrom of deepening financial despair.

I was awaiting two events: the signal from the hospital to join my wife Karen, who was expecting our second child – the reason for our brief return to England – and the arrival of my good friend and High Court claimant, Ron. I was accompanied by Julie, a dear friend of many years, who would sit for our first child, Emily, in the house that we had borrowed from holidaying friends as Karen approached the decisive moment. Ron had rung me a few hours earlier.

'Ben? You'll never guess what! They've reached an out-of-court settlement. We're there! I'll be with you in an hour.'

Ron was a cartoonist. The best I'd seen after seventeen years in the art business. He had designed publicity cartoon characters for leading companies across the world, and was now nearing the close of a horrible, drawn-out case against one of America's biggest fast-food corporations. They had been using his work without permission and, as reported in the broadsheets, were now being sued by his major London law firm for over a million pounds for copyright infringement. We had backed him all the way; a support based on a mutual dislike for tyrants and instinctive siding with the underdog.

I recall the first time I had seen Ron: a huge bear of a man, with a great mane of long, thick, slightly greying hair, enormous sky-blue eyes and the warmest, widest smile I could remember. He was immensely genuine, open and charismatic. He had walked into the high-street gallery that I'd been running for several years in Norwich and I was immediately drawn to his openness. He ordered several frames to be made for the latest restaurant he had refurbished for the fast-food chain and spent a while admiring the artworks on the walls. Within fifteen minutes of his entering the building, we were discussing philosophy, life and all its diversity. We became instant friends.

A year or two later, following a continued business and personal friendship, he called me at the gallery. The tone of his voice told me that there was something amiss.

'Hi, Ben. Can you meet me this evening after work? Anywhere you like, I just need to talk to someone. The Fat Cat? Fantastic, my friend! We'll need a glass or two methinks. See you there, say, at seven? Thanks so much, Ben.'

The Fat Cat has won numerous awards for its ridiculous variety of real beer in outstanding condition, and was located just two doors from our house at the time. It was a superb choice of venue for such a rendezvous, as it lay directly in my path as I approached the house after a long day at the gallery. Karen would often call me if I had been working late and, hearing the merry chink of glasses and jolly conversation in the background, would sarcastically remark:

'In the "office" again? Oh well, maybe you'll make the last twenty yards home before too long, then...'

On occasions such as this, staggering home some four hours later, I would attempt to mollify her with a take-away carton of Enville Ginger or Rawalpindi IPA, but I stood about as much chance of success as a fish in a rock-climbing competition.

As I sipped my ale of choice, Ron entered the pub, and I observed in an instant the uncharacteristic drawn expression written across his face. We found a quiet corner – thank God for pubs designed for those still wishing to engage in that quaint pastime, conversation – and, drinks in place, Ron fired a direct question at me.

'Ben, what do you think of the fast-food business?'

I hesitated. Multinational corporations, with all their disrespect for the average employee, glorifying maximum profits for those at the top, at the expense of the people who actually create their fortunes down below, had always been anathema to me. On the other hand, I had been receiving regular orders from Ron as a direct result of his contract with them and therefore had to consider carefully the income it generated for my family. My answer came within a second of his question.

'I hate everything it stands for,' I replied.

A broad smile crept across his now jolly face, as he said:

'My friend, I love you!'

He then commenced a tale of such outrageous commercial brutality that, unless I had known the man for two years and trusted him implicitly, I would not have believed a word of it. In order to minimise costs, the fast-food chain UK had approached him in an attempt to buy the rights to all his drawings. The unlimited use of his work would save them a fortune in the long run, as they were presently paying Ron, a sound businessman himself, each time they used it in every new restaurant or refurbishment. Ron declined the offer, stating firmly that his work was his property and would remain so. Now, the fact that not everyone has a price was a difficult concept for the Americans to come to terms with and, when several attempts to persuade him to change his mind had met with the same steel-calm response, a dark day dawned in the history of commercial foul play.

Ron entered his offices one morning to find no staff, no computers and no CD archive, on which his work had been stored for years. It appeared that the company had been infiltrated, employees had been blackmailed, and his work of several years had been simply stolen from under his nose. Such a blatant disregard for ethics, fuelled by the arrogant omnipotence that immense wealth engenders, plumbed the depths of the commercialist cesspit.

Reeling in disbelief, Ron consulted his London law firm, where he had always registered the copyrights for his drawings. It was an open and shut case. As his new work continued to be used across the world, with none of the usual payments forthcoming, the firm uniquely offered their services on a "No Win, No Fee" basis, so certain were they of the result. The only problem was keeping Ron afloat from day-to-day during the two years or so that would ensue before a likely date in the High Court would deliver compensation. For technical reasons, it was essential that he did not become bankrupt along the way. And he had a home, wife and young son of twelve to support while he prepared his case against the multinational behemoth.

As we started on our third pints, my eyes continued to widen as Ron recounted further details of this increasingly shocking story. He told me of the anonymous and threatening phone calls, telling him to drop the case. He told me of the misty autumn morning, when he discovered the message scrawled across his windscreen: "WE ALWAYS KNOW WHERE YOU ARE". He told me of the early-morning knock on his back door, when he calmly and quietly told his wife and son to stand near the front door, ready to run in the event of any menacing developments. He had opened the back door to find two huge men, armed with baseball bats, flattened against the wall, either side of the doorframe. Ron's inherent fortitude, inner calm and eloquence saved the day. Ten minutes later, they were sharing a pot of tea with him in his kitchen.

The final, and most terrifying, attempt to dissuade him from battling on against the enemy again utilised an unknown voice over the telephone. By this time, Ron had managed to have his phone bugged in order to build an absolutely watertight body of evidence against those that were endeavouring to engineer his demise. The flat, emotionless voice coldly told him to drop the case.

'I suggest you don't continue with this action,' it said.

'I will not stop my quest for justice, my friend,' replied Ron.

'Then I suggest that it's not safe for young boys of twelve to be outside of their home for as long as you continue.'

How on earth Ron remained sane throughout this period is an indication of the infinite inner strength of the man; a strength which, in turn, inspired in me a steely determination to reveal, at all costs, the horrible corruption lying behind seemingly harmless everyday commerce. The more he told me, the more I began to understand the huge power of international business interests. Such massive corporations are not only beyond the law. They are the law. They are the financial phantoms pulling the strings of the political puppets, those faceless marionettes that jump and dance to the tune played by their megalomaniac masters.

The usual bar-room crowd became a hazy blur as I struggled to find a straw of humanity amongst this money-driven world system to which I could cling. I needed to find someone, somewhere, who could reinstall something of the belief in human nature and integrity that I had always maintained.

The person was standing right in front of me. And he needed help.

'How much do you need?' I asked.

Over the following two years, our dedication to the cause of truth and justice drew us together into a deeper and more profound friendship than any I had experienced. We became absolutely determined that the world would hear of the dark and slimy practices driving big business, and Karen and I decided that, whatever the cost, the fight had to realise its ultimate fulfilment in the High Court. The family business was moderately successful and we were able, at regular intervals, to continue to assist Ron along the long road towards justice.

I recall the day that we travelled to meet his lawyers in London. I had rarely seen such an impressive and imposing monolith of a building as the offices of the firm, which lay within a few hundred yards of St Paul's Cathedral. We had experienced a difficult few months, during which we had just managed, between us, to keep the wolves of repossession from the door of Ron's small family house. After strolling through the corridors of his legal advocates, however, I was imbued with a huge sense of confidence in those who were fighting for us. With such an eminent international concern collating incontrovertible evidence daily, I finally knew that only time separated Ron and the world from the day of truth.

And now the time had come. The High Court hearing was to take place on Monday, June the 30th, 2003. The timing was a providential coincidence. We had left England on the first of May for a new life in the south of France, Karen being seven months pregnant at the time of our departure. Having installed the family in a small village apartment, we had spent a month and a half overseeing the initiation of the construction of our mountain home; the result of eight years' planning. We had returned to Norwich during June for the birth of our second child, since Karen's medical and maternity history was still with our English doctors, and were loaned the use of a house during our stay by friends of long standing. And so it came about that we were to be back in England to witness also the result of our two-and-a-half-year campaign against one of the most powerful commercial enterprises the world has ever seen. Karen's labour was proving to be a drawn-out affair, and I was back at the house with little Emily and Julie when Ron called me with the news of the settlement.

Since his lawyers had offered to fight the case on a "No Win, No Fee" basis, they apparently had the prerogative to accept or refuse any offer forthcoming from the other side in an attempt to prevent the hearing going ahead in the courtroom. It was obviously a reasonable settlement, otherwise Ron's lawyers would have insisted on seeing the business out in court the following day. I recalled having seen, just a few weeks earlier, the small article in one of the broadsheets, reporting the fact that Ron was suing the fast-food chain in the High Court for at least a seven-figure sum. The figure itself was, of course, meaningless, for not only had Ron suffered the loss of a business, an income and the outright theft of all that he had created, but he and his small family had also been subjected to a campaign of terror for more than two years. The extreme nature of this campaign had shocked all who were associated with its results, and had left emotional scars which no amount of money could remove.

Having heard his news on that dark, damp and cloudy evening, I was relieved that at last his nightmare was over, but admittedly somewhat peeved that the matter had been settled before the revolting details of the case could be exposed to the general public; such exposure had been our driving motivation all along. As I heard a car turn into the street, I experienced a sense of nauseous expectation. Over the previous six weeks, we had been prey to an unimaginable run of bad luck, and had returned to England with the whole French project teetering on the edge of a financial abyss. Now, as the sound of Ron's feet upon the gravel matched my own along the hall carpet, I felt positive that what he was about to tell me would finally make all things well.

I opened the door before his finger reached the bell, and it seemed as if the incessant, damp gloom swirled into the hall along with my friend. However, despite the murk of despair that had surrounded us for so long, I knew we were finally about to cross the threshold of hope.

Chapter 2

May the first had seen us packing all the possessions we would need for a furnished apartment into two cars totally unfit for the purpose. We owned at the time a small BMW saloon of sixteen years' vintage, and my old Panther, a two-seater eccentricity and Morgan substitute, far less valuable but considerably more powerful. Due to its almost comical power to weight ratio, driving the Panther was akin to piloting some sort of bionic roller skate, its rear-wheel drive rendering it lethal on anything but the driest of surfaces, and in a straight line. The man who had sold it to me some eight years earlier had wryly commented on the day of purchase:

'Start her up, hit the gas and let rip. If you can pull away with a straight face, she's yours for nothing.'

Fat chance. As I floored the accelerator my face was split with the biggest grin since God ended Adam's frustration by turning a boring bone into a willing woman.

The majority of our household contents had been concertinaed into the council garage we were renting a hundred yards down the road. With the contract clearly stating that it was to be used for the sole purpose of garaging a vehicle, and categorically not for the use of indefinite furniture storage by an unhinged family about to flee the country, we were flaunting all clauses of the rental agreement. But needs must and, mentally justifying the action by recalling that I had never missed any local authority charges since I'd first left home some twenty years earlier, I paid the amazingly reasonable rent for the following six months in advance and locked away our worldly goods until the house we were about to build was sufficiently completed to accept the transferral of its future contents.

The two cars packed to the hilt with basic clothes, bedding, kitchen utensils and other paraphernalia, we spent our final hours as Norwich residents sipping farewell pints outside the Fat Cat along with two of the many good friends we were sadly leaving behind.

Julie was tearful as we said our goodbyes. Our first child, Emily, then nearly three years old, adored her. She was also highly respected by Francesca, Karen's daughter from a previous relationship, in whose upbringing I'd had the pleasure of sharing for the eight years since I had met her mother. Francesca was now approaching twelve years of age and was spending some time in the Canary Islands with Karen's parents, planning to re-join the family when we returned to Norwich at the time of the new baby's arrival two months later. Little Emily was about to embark on the longest car journey of her short life.

Also there to see us on our way was Ian, our mechanic, who had spent the previous few days readying the vehicles for the long trek to the far south-eastern corner of France.

'Thair'll mairke it oilroight,' he had informed me drily in his rich Norwich brogue, 'but Oi caarn't say as thee'll larst much larnger 'n thaat, ol' boy. People will be insistin' arn droivin' heaps o' shit, Oi s'poose.'

Ian, dear Ian. The son of Norfolk parents – his father tall and lean, his mother a cuddly four feet six – Ian was built like a disproportionate bulldog. Legs like oaks supported a great, muscular torso, topped by a neck at least as broad as its shaved head. A wild assortment of gold rings, necklaces and earrings completed the frightful appearance of a bodybuilding pirate. Always accompanied by his faithful Doberman, Rommel, Ian's favourite pastime was to drive, as if they were fairground bumper cars, one of a series of vintage Rolls-Royces which he was forever restoring in his garage workshops. There was many a summer evening when he would rocket past the pub searching for a parking space, refusing to slow down for speed bumps in the narrow street, while the wonderfully capable suspension of the vehicle retained the car's perfect horizontality as car and driver were bounced two feet into the air in front of us. One particular evening, he had handed the keys to Ron, who had met me for a drink during hard times. Ian observed a man who needed cheering up and told him, without question or concern for the car, to take his young son for a spin in the Roller while we drank to their health. Dear old Ian: loud, proud, strong, generous. And gay. We loved him to bits.

The tears were flowing all round as we finally started up the cars and set off on our way. A time of such extreme catharsis is incredibly difficult to describe to another individual: one's entire collection of personal life experiences distilled into a single, uniquely fulfilling moment. It seemed as if my whole life up to that point had been some sort of preparation, a crazy and varied thirty-nine years, the thirty-nine steps to the launch of a new existence across a far horizon. I found it hard to believe that, after many years of dreaming, planning and shaping our lives to this single day of realisation, the time was actually now, as, for the final time, I gunned the engine and headed south, towards London and beyond.

That evening we had arranged to stay overnight at my sister's house in a beautiful Kentish village just outside Canterbury, allowing us an early start to catch the Channel Tunnel link to France first thing the next morning. Alison and Danny had always been magnanimously hospitable, given the doll's-house proportions of their quaint village mews residence, and were pleased to be of help on the final leg of our flight from the country. Alison and Karen offered to cook a meal, while Danny asked if I would like a final taste of an English pub; a cosy, friendly hostelry being within fifty yards of their house.

We told the girls we'd be back shortly: five pints and three hours later, we were somewhat confused at the short shrift we received on our return. Nevertheless, the evening continued in a celebratory and reminiscent manner, and we finally fell into our makeshift beds far later than we had previously envisaged.

It seemed as though I had hardly fallen asleep before Alison was pressing a strong cup of tea into my hand in an attempt to rouse me from what felt like the bottom of a Guinness-soaked swamp. The importance of the day finally dawned across my befuddled mind, so I quickly rose and made ready for our final departure from English soil. We were waved on our way with promises of a visit as soon as we had got ourselves organised in France, and arrived at the Tunnel with plenty of time to spare before the next crossing.

Before we had left Norwich, I had made some enquiries as to times and costs of a one-way car crossing by ferry, tunnel and hovercraft. It seemed that the best deal was by ferry, albeit a lot slower, of course, until one day, while reading through a promotional brochure I had been sent by the Channel Tunnel people, I spotted a loophole in the pricing. A one-way journey by car (we were not, of course, intending to return) with contents and passengers was around £140, but they were offering, at the same time, a "Day Return" special deal for shoppers, at just £25 per car. We bought two such tickets with their "same day return" counterparts at the terminal, saving £230 and getting, into the bargain, two return tickets, never to be used, and which we still have as souvenirs of our departure to this very day. What on earth the ticket inspector thought we were doing going across the Channel for one day, driving cars loaded to explosive proportions, with the tarpaulin-covered mountain on the roof of the BMW almost taller than the car itself, is anyone's guess, but amazingly, it wasn't queried.

As we drove off the train at the other end and climbed the ramp towards the French "autoroute" heading south, I attempted to film the moment with a camcorder held just above the steering wheel.

Suddenly, however, I was again overcome with an intensely clear awareness, the knowledge that we had left the country for the last time, and that we had radically and irrevocably altered our lives and those of our children. This was accompanied by a great wave of emotional release, a sense of new life, rebirth almost, and I wept profusely.

"That was the river," I thought, in the words of one of the Waterboys' most inspiring songs, "This is the sea!"

Chapter 3

For anyone who has not had the privilege of driving on French autoroutes, the first time elicits a progressive series of gasps and sighs as one takes in the enormous differences from the English motorway system. One is shocked at the lack of traffic, the absolute absence of roadworks, the unblemished, smooth surfaces. And the most encouraging thing of all is that, in the Western world, a road system unencumbered by endless, redundant lines of traffic cones in the outside lane, with no visible reason for their existence for miles on end, actually exists. I have often wondered as to the pervasive presence of these mystery cones of no apparent purpose, and the phantom roadworks that one expects to come across at some point along their course, but which never seem to materialise. Ben Elton finally gave me the answer I was searching for when I recently found time to read his excellent novel, *Gridlock*. I recommend it to all who wring their hands in despair as to the state of the English highways.

The long drive south was punctuated by only two events of note.

We had managed, somehow, to cover three quarters of the journey virtually within sight of one another: Karen and Emily sang the *Rosie and Jim* theme tune to distract our poor daughter from the interminable stretches of tarmac ahead, while I, in the Panther, constantly endeavoured to absolutely not use its incredible powers of acceleration when confronted by road users I would rather leave behind. We had thus maintained visual contact of each other for eight hundred kilometres of the journey, until the dawning of one bright day which saw us leaving our second stop, at Avignon.

As we exited the town, an alarmingly complex road system tried its best to thwart us from our course. Driving slowly, I just about managed to keep Karen in my rear-view mirror despite the hordes of local, teenage speedsters that were shifting lanes at a pace they presumably thought sufficient to impress road users of greater experience.

Oh dear. Poor Karen was lost behind some screaming adolescent with something to prove, while I slowed as much as I could so that she wouldn't lose sight of me, and the way out of town, ahead. Glancing into my rear-view mirror as I approached the slip lane on to the autoroute, I realised that she was no longer in sight, and decided to pull over on to the hard shoulder in order to call her on the mobile and reaffirm our relative positions.

Oh fuck. The battery was dead. And the autoroute patrol was fast-approaching as I looked behind me. Here I was, illegally parked on the side of a foreign motorway, unable to communicate with my wife and child who, as far as I knew, had no idea of the way ahead, wondering if they would ever find their way out of the medieval road system to follow me on to the autoroute, and now being targeted by the state highway patrol, slowly approaching and already shouting that I had to clear the lane, when suddenly, tyres squealing as she exited the slip road in an amazing display of navigational prowess, Karen swarmed past me and onwards, slowing slightly as I finally caught up with her driving ability and presence of mind.

As we commenced the third and last leg of the journey towards our destination, the countryside became savage in both scale and colour. Grey skies became a shimmering blue, grey rocks changed to red and, although we were approaching the Mediterranean, the fierce greenery of pine and wild oak took us by breathless surprise.

There was a whole other-worldliness about this landscape; the almost unbearable brightness contributing to a sense that time really stood still here, that anything could happen, and that the rest of the planet would know nothing about it. I finally understood why Van Gogh had gone crazy in this part of the world: the wind, the sun, the colour, the clarity; the absolute intensity of all visual reality closes in so as to almost suffocate with its effervescent presence.

And on the autoroute, a different magic was playing its game. We were halfway between Aix and Cannes when a white van screamed past me at an improbable speed, swerving left and right as it shot ahead. I couldn't believe its ridiculous trajectory, and slowed automatically. It also slowed, matching my speed, and, drawing alongside, the driver shouted something to me, something about the Panther being a "pretty" car. I daintily swerved from his dangerous proximity, and shouted 'Merci, et bonne journée!' as he accelerated back into the middle of the road.

A central concrete barrier about a metre in height runs the length of the autoroute in these parts, and I was given a blindingly obvious demonstration of the need for it at that point in time, as the van rocketed ahead and sidelong into the concrete wall, sparks flying while the driver struggled to come to terms with his lunchtime quotient of pastis. In an effort to prove to the world that he wasn't actually as pissed as the proverbial fart, he continued to hug the central reservation, bouncing off it at regular intervals until all traffic in his wake had slowed to allow him on his way, thankfully without harm to them, but to cause goodness knows what mayhem to those who lay before him.

We covered the final, and most scenically spectacular, leg of the journey in a somewhat more sedate fashion. After all, as the majestic megaliths of the Alpes-Maritimes grew ever larger on the horizon, the village of Gréolières, and our new home, was now only a few hours away.

Chapter 4

I had first discovered the village of Gréolières some eight years previously, shortly before I made the acquaintance of my second wife-to-be, Karen. I'd just completed a course in paragliding in the Peak District, and the south-eastern corner of France had been recommended as an ideal location in which to develop my burgeoning skills, Gréolières being not only a classic flying site but also easily accessible from Nice Airport.

As I exited the Gorges du Loup (Wolf River Gorge) for the first time, and the valley in which the village was situated opened panoramically before my eyes, I was not only absolutely awestruck by its verdant beauty but also, in that very moment, overcome by an irrational, but utterly unequivocal, sense of homecoming. I somehow knew that I would live there; not as a conscious decision, but rather more of a comfortable realisation that what had always been the case had just been revealed to me. Perhaps it was something to do with the bizarre familiarity of the landscape. As children, my parents would often take us camping in the English Lake District, and many happy family memories from my childhood are set, in the cinema of my mind, against a backdrop of green-swathed mountains, rivers and lakes. Perhaps it was the vision of the sublime valley in which I now found myself that jolted forth hitherto forgotten emotions of happiness and security.

An indication of the nature of the landscape in this region is first offered to the visitor from the left-hand window of an aircraft, when flying south towards the promontory that forms the landing strip at Nice Airport. The second busiest airport in the country is cleverly designed so as to keep all aircraft out to sea on approach and take-off, preserving, to some extent, the sanity of the local Niçois. In the east, on a clear day, one can see the continuously snow-clad pyramids of the Alps, gradually decreasing in scale as they sweep in a graceful curve towards the Mediterranean, forming a natural boundary between France and Italy. These are the Maritime Alps.

The mountains meet the sea in a confusion of deep-green valleys, their inherent inaccessibility having prevented the scars created by the Riviera cities from penetrating too hideously into the beautiful countryside inland. Fifteen minutes after leaving the airport, therefore, one finds oneself winding gently uphill along rock-lined lanes, surrounded on all sides by a panoply of plant life, enough of it familiar enough to make even the most ardent anglophile feel at home.

The roads between Nice and Gréolières are a revelation for anyone moved by the grandeur of wild mountain terrain. The route most often used to reach the village threads its way through a spectacular river canyon, the limestone having been eroded over thousands of years by the Wolf River, which rushes along its floor, clear and blue beneath cliff-hanging trees on its way to the sea. On a hot day, the traveller can stop at one of the numerous pools for a cooling swim, the paths and small beaches still unspoilt by the barriers, gates and fences one would expect to find in modern, litigation-loopy England.

As one continues northwards, with the road consistently climbing as it leaves the gorge behind, the immense east-west rock wall of the massif du Cheiron rises magnificently into view. This mountain, on whose southern flank is situated the village where we were to later make our home, provides the valley with shelter from the north. It also forms, with the sea in the south, a natural sanctuary from the elements, and a mild microclimate in which the sun shines for well over three hundred days of the year. The village itself, perched on an outcrop at an altitude of eight hundred and fifty metres was, at one time, the main Roman outpost between Vence and Castellane, and retains numerous physical reminders of its rich and colourful history to this day.

Having introduced Karen to the area a year after I had first come across it, and hoping to impress my “paragliding widow” for ulterior motives, we found that on each occasion we visited the valley for holidays or weekend breaks we discovered something else to recommend it as an environment in which to make a home. The very fact that a place of such dramatically unspoilt natural beauty happened to be only forty minutes from an airport serving the budget airlines was of great importance when considering the convenience of visiting relatives. The village also housed a new school, with a bus service to the city of Grasse for older students, and therefore presented no educational difficulties for the children.

There were delightful mountain walks from the doorstep, the seasons followed a precise pattern, there was skiing to be had on the north side of the mountain in winter, there were lakes, rivers, and, of course, the Mediterranean beaches for swimming. And most importantly of all, the locals were cheerful, helpful and accepting of foreigners (I could only hope that a non-English-speaking Frenchman would fare equally well when hoping to make his home in a rural Norfolk village of three hundred and fifty souls ...). Oh, and of course the wine was cheap and plentiful.

The more we became acquainted with Gréolières, the more we wanted to stay there for good and, after numerous brief visits, it appeared that there was only one small thing to be considered before upping and leaving England for our personal nirvana: how on earth were we going to make a living?

I have often mused as to the rather strange way that we, in the West, meekly accept that it is the fate of modern man to spend the majority of the short time we are given on this planet working, often in unfavourable surroundings, at a task that offers little or no satisfaction on a personal or social level. To what end? In order to amount such material wealth that we are able to buy endless sundry items which we don't want or need, but that the great marketing machine of the world has convinced us are necessary for happiness.

On the other hand, we were of the conviction that what was going to make us and our children happy, first and foremost, was a peaceful location in which to live, surrounded by a social network of good friends, and with the time to spend doing things that were worthy of our attention during the short period we have on this earth.

One of the most useful things that anyone has ever said to me was, 'Ben, you know what? Life's not about collecting things. It's about collecting experiences.' Advice for life indeed. I knew that living in a friendly community, in which crime was still virtually unheard of, and in which our children were free to roam in one of the most beautiful natural locations I had seen, would, in itself, offer abundant chances for collecting new experiences. And so we decided that what we were going to do was to find a way to make enough money to live at a modest level, releasing the rest of our lives to spend with the children and each other, in the enjoyment of the stunning region in which we proposed to live.

The answer, of course, was sitting under our noses. If we had been so taken by the area ourselves, having returned again and again for all it had to offer, then surely others too would want to spend their holidays here. We would run a guesthouse, and make a living from sharing our wonderful discovery with like-minded folk from far and wide. It was a sound decision based on several years of research into the variety of activities available locally.

Apart from being a paragliding and hang-gliding mecca, there was a miscellany of other things to do for people of both an active and less sporting disposition. Rock-climbing, canyoning, horse-riding, mountain walking, caving, archery and, of course, everything associated with a winter ski station were all within a few kilometres of where we intended to make our home. Although, like myself, I also felt sure that there were those who would appreciate nothing more than a warm climate, wild and bewitching scenery, peace and quiet, a good book and a glass of fine wine or three. We became convinced, after the time we had devoted to getting to know the place ourselves, that we had found the answer. And so our search for a suitable, and affordable, house began.

We spent a couple of years returning time and again to various estate agents scattered throughout the regional towns and villages.

But, finding nothing that was A) fit for the purpose, and B) within the price range we could afford if we sold everything we owned in England, we became despondent. It was beginning to dawn on me that although we had found a place in which to live, breathe and prosper, there was, as ever, a high price to pay. In fact, it was at about this time we learned that, apart from Paris itself, this was the most expensive corner of this vast country in which to purchase property.

And the more we ventured farther from the valley, desperately searching for cheaper options in the mountains further to the north, east and west, the more we absolutely knew that the only place we felt at home was Gréolières. Here, in the place we had already adopted as home within our hearts, we realised that there was nothing to be had, and even had it existed at all, it was going to be totally out of reach of our meagre financial capability.

And then finally, as despondency turned into despair, we met serendipity in the form of Pierre and Monique.

Chapter 5

We had spent a last-ditch house-hunting week based in the extremely comfortable Chambres d'hôtes owned by Pierre and Monique Delgrange, just three hundred metres from Gréolières village centre.

They had built their house with their own bare hands, which inspired in me a new determination to reach our goal at a time when it seemed the walls of failure were closing in on us. They were special people; a more amicable couple one couldn't wish to meet. Monique's sparkling elfin beauty, and Pierre's capacity to utilise every muscle in his face to create a smile of the most heart-warming proportions, could not fail to impress even the coldest of visitors to their cosy hostelry.

They spent the week observing our forays into the hopeless wilderness of the various estate agents' promised lands of milk and honey. Realising that we were ending our stay in a far more depressed mood than the one of optimism with which we had arrived, they finally sat down for a serious chat with us a day or two before our return to England.

It transpired that they had been happy to meet us, that they already counted us as friends, and that having watched, at close quarters, our relentless quest for a place to call our own, they wanted to suggest a solution. The piece of land bordering theirs, and within five minutes' walk of the village centre, was for sale. Had we thought about building the house we needed, rather than trying to find an existing one that just happened to meet our requirements? No, we had not, and neither did we know of land for sale in the area. Such local knowledge is the result of being accepted and spoken to; we were privileged to have stumbled upon it. I felt hopelessly flattered that, having spent less than a week in their company, these wonderful people had given us the information that could make us their next-door neighbours for the rest of their lives. I was moved beyond words to have made such marvellous friends as this, in the place I had come to love with a passion. Things were finally falling into place.

Pierre kindly explained to us where the owner of the land lived, some six or seven kilometres along the wooded road which wound its way along the bottom of the valley. It seemed to be the case that the Martin family owned many small pieces of land in and around the village but, due to French inheritance laws, rarely managed to arrive at the point of sale when attempting to profit from their legacy.

In France, all children, along with the mother, current wife, or wives, depending on the extent of the traditional shenanigans entered into by the father, can have an equal right of inheritance, unless specifically stated otherwise in the will. This is, one presumes, extant in order to prevent the situation in which a new wife automatically becomes the next of kin and leaves other women's children high and dry at the time of their father's death.

However, it also leads to absurdly complex states of affairs, especially in the case of inherited land. There are many instances in which, due to endless bickering by the children, now well into old age themselves, no agreements can be arrived at with respect to the sale price of a family plot. Or, indeed, whether it should be sold at all, but rather left to their own, more numerous children, the arguments then becoming too convoluted to warrant consideration or stand any chance of becoming resolved.

It appeared, then, that we were astonishingly fortunate, not only to have found some land that was possibly for sale, but over which no family feud was still underway.

With only a day of our stay remaining, I packed Karen and Emily, then just eighteen months old, into the car and shot off in the direction of the Martins' farmhouse. The French love children, and I was cynically hoping to employ my winsome young daughter's presence as a counterbalance for my incredibly crude handling of the French language. It was about this time that I started to regret having chosen German as a modern language when attending high school. Even though I had spent the last year and a half at a French evening class for adults, in what I saw as responsible preparation for our impending emigration, my stomach lurched as we rounded a bend in the road and their house came into view.

I knew that what we were about to initiate was a potentially pivotal course of events, for which we were not fully prepared. I could hardly speak the lingo, the local accent rendered even the most simple of replies beyond rational comprehension, I had not yet acquainted myself with all the legal requirements in connection with land purchase in this new country, and I had a family whose future could depend on the next half hour of my life. It couldn't have felt worse to be entering the ring at a Spanish bullfight, unarmed and wearing a freshly-tailored scarlet three-piece suit.

Wary at first, old Madame Martin's face relaxed once she knew why she had been visited by these madly-grinning, nervous foreigners, and she invited us into the cosy farmhouse kitchen to meet her ageing and frail husband, Gaston. Dust was blown off ancient deeds and manuscripts, maps were laid out on the old wooden table, and a terrifying few minutes ensued, during which my earlier fears of non-comprehension became a horrifying reality. This was terrible: I was picking up about one word in ten, and beginning to think things were hopeless, until Gaston made the whole thing simpler by proffering a piece of paper with a large number on it and offering us a glass of their newly-brewed orange wine. Suddenly, all became clear: this was the price of the land, and the wine was there to soften us into drunk acceptance.

It rather reminded me of our preview evenings at the gallery back in Norwich, when free wine would be given to all and sundry in the futile hope that at least some of the guests would see the paintings in a new and desirable light. Of course it rarely worked, so the remainder of the night's booze would disappear in a wild celebration of the fact that at least we'd had a great evening and made lots of new friends, whether or not anything had been sold. It was probably the fact that I enjoyed the socialising more than the selling that finally led to my ultimate disillusionment in the field of business, but there were some wonderful parties nonetheless.

Inspired by the soothing warmth of the delicious, and unbeknown to us at the time, fortified wine, I started to feel somewhat more confident. I trusted Pierre, these were honest country folk, and the price of sixty thousand euros for three thousand square metres of perfectly situated land seemed more than reasonable. I asked what we should do next.

A quick phone call brought their cousin from the village, as it was he who handled matters of a legal nature for the family. By the time he arrived, we were on our third glass of wine and in celebratory mood. He was going to handle everything, he explained in words that I was suddenly able to understand (was it the alcohol that had released the chains of linguistic torpor from my clouded brain?); all we had to do would be to return the next day, the morning of the day we returned to England, and he would arrange for the *notaire* to be present so that all could be finalised before we left the country. We were jubilant as we made our way back to Pierre's guesthouse in the village. We hadn't the words to thank him for his beneficence. The land was practically ours.

That evening, Pierre's friend, Michel, dropped in to share an aperitif with the couple.

Aperitifs in this part of the world are not, as one may presume, a small drink to whet one's appetite before starting the day's main meal. It seems that the lunchtime wine has only just come to an end when people start mentioning the word "aperitif", in vague reference to the continuation of the day's consumption of alcohol. The understanding of the word "aperitif" could be roughly translated as:

'Mmm, nice lunch; er, what's the time? Half three, you say? Well, anyone fancy a few glasses of a little something before we head for the pub for some pastis in advance of the restaurant tonight?'

We were introduced to Michel as Pierre began to pour the first of a series of glasses of pastis. Michel was, it amazingly transpired, not only an architect, but also happened to live right there in Gréolières! Pierre suggested we talk to him about the land we were on the point of purchasing before we left for home and we eagerly accepted, as I began to wonder whether we were becoming the centre of some bizarre conspiracy to provide jobs for the boys throughout the region. As Michel discussed ideas with us, he suddenly said, 'It's a shame you're not here longer. I've got some land for sale as well and it would have been nice to show it to you. In fact, it's only over the road – do you want to have a look?'

We were both extremely tired by this point and knew that we couldn't possibly find a better site for our project than the one we were about to sign for in the morning. Nevertheless, I decided to humour the chap, as his land was in such close proximity. Karen chose to stay and relax with Pierre and Monique, content that our week's work had been done.

Half an hour later, I returned to Pierre's place and told Karen that I had changed my mind.

'What?' she exclaimed. 'At this point? I thought everything had been decided!'

'It had been,' I sighed in response, 'but I've seen something better ...'

Using every faculty of persuasion I possessed, I now endeavoured to sell her Michel's piece of land. The view was better, I explained, and because it was below the road rather than above, there was no traffic noise.

'But there's only about three cars a day that pass here!' she knowingly replied.

I then described the situation of the other plot, being more spectacular as it occupied a wild and steep part of the mountainside.

'More difficult to build on,' she correctly observed.

I played my trump card.

'He's offered to do the plans for nothing if we buy his land,' I manically blurted, 'and it's ten grand cheaper to boot!'

I was huffing and puffing, and Karen's defence collapsed like the house of the first little pig.

We made plans with Michel to return soon and tie up the purchase of his site, but now, with our plane leaving the following day and the expectant sellers at the house of Martin arranging a rendezvous with their solicitor before our departure, we were in a sticky situation.

It's at times like this that one hopes one is able to summon one's strength, lay one's cards on the table and be honest, straight and direct in explaining one's change of course face to face ...

So twenty minutes later found Karen furtively creeping up to the door of the farmhouse, cop-out letter in hand, hoping there would be a crack wide enough to slip it under without disturbing the drowsy cats, dogs and chickens, while I slunk behind the dashboard of our hired car at the foot of the drive, engine idling for a quick getaway.

It was to be more than a year before Monsieur Martin's cousin deemed us worthy of even the slightest recognition on the roads of the village.

Chapter 6

The concluding months of 2002 and the spring of 2003 had seen us in frenzied activity between Norwich and Nice, arranging the final purchase of Michel's land and finding a builder to start the work for us. Michel had managed to organise planning permission for a house, along with a small block containing a garage and rooms to let, without too much trouble, as he had previously obtained outline permission for the property before divorcing his wife and thus being compelled to sell his land.

The completion of the acquisition of the terrain involved a particularly bizarre day in which we left Norwich at four o'clock in the morning, returning at ten o'clock the same evening. Babysitting and other considerations had necessitated an absence of minimum duration, so the signing of the documents in the *notaire's* offices in Cannes was followed by a hasty, celebratory lunch, bought for us by Michel at a small restaurant overlooking the sun-drenched beach close by. We felt exuberant as we returned on the plane during the early evening and celebrated with a bottle of in-flight champagne, ignoring, for once, its outrageously-concocted, captive-audience price. After all, this occasion was truly special.

It was strange to be driving back up the A11 from Stansted in cold fog just a few hours later. Thank God for the arrival of low-cost airlines.

By December, we had sold the gallery business and had received a quote for the building work from Gary, a builder who had lived in France for eleven years and who had been recommended by a good friend of mine. We had no wish to offend the locals by utilising foreign labour, but as Gary had been there for so long, and therefore, we assumed, had integrated well enough with the locals to be on good terms with all, we went along to see the house that he had built for himself. Just twenty minutes down the road from the location of our new land, it was hugely impressive, tastefully utilising reclaimed materials throughout and, given our still weak knowledge of the language, we decided that we were justified in employing an Englishman in this instance. We gave him copies of the plans and agreed a monthly wage for him and the two labourers he would need to construct the admittedly large dwelling within the timescale we hoped would see the commencement of our letting business: approximately a year.

The family had endured an incredibly difficult eighteen months up to this point, involving complications with house sales, business sales, stress induced by the High Court episode, and inter-personal conflicts leading to near-affairs and other threats to our family and financial security. The nadir of this period saw me seeking regular refuge in narcotics in an attempt to escape the huge pressure of the changes I had dreamed of, but whose realisation was at times becoming simply too stressful to carry through. But now, with things in France slowly coming together and the date of Ron's court case having been fixed for the 30th of June, we felt sure we could detect a glimmer at the end of a long, long, tunnel.

And so began the darkest year of our lives.

We decided to use the following twelve months to concentrate on rebuilding our relationship while the work got underway in France, without the problems created in a family when one or other of the partners is working at least six days out of seven, and long days at that.

The first bombshell came out of the blue as the phone rang one fine spring morning. It was Gary.

'Er, Ben, this house is gonna cost about a hundred thousand euros more than we first thought.'

My life, my hopes and dreams, my future, my universe, all ebbed and flowed as a psychedelic tidal wave of fear crashed on to the shores of my disbelieving consciousness.

'Oh, fuck,' was all I could manage to say, as my vital organs seemed to fly out of my body and perform gory gyrations before my very eyes. 'Why?'

'Well, I've had another look at the plans and they're not to scale or something. I can't do it for the price, I'm afraid.'

Retrospectively, it turned out that the new price was realistic, but I never quite understood how the design had managed to be so drastically misunderstood in the first place.

'Any suggestions?' I meekly replied, ignoring, for some reason, the cacophonous pealing of warning bells within my head.

'Yeah, if you want to build the thing with the money you got, yer gonna 'ave to get over 'ere and take the place of one of the builders.'

Five years earlier I would have leapt at the chance to build our own home, but after recent events, I was not in good shape, mentally or physically. I doubted whether I had the strength left in me for this.

'OK,' I said, 'find me somewhere to rent nearby and we'll move as soon as we can,' as I saw our restorative year dissolve into twelve months of hard labour.

Karen, as ever, provided the huge moral support and encouragement that I needed. After a hurriedly-arranged sale of the tiny terraced house we had moved into after taking the profit on our family home to fund progress in France, we had four weeks to get used to the idea that we would be quitting English soil on the first of May.

We planned to leave the majority of the money we had managed to accumulate in England, since, just after the launch of the euro across Europe, the pound had weakened somewhat, and I felt sure that it would regain its strength over the coming months as the novelty of the new currency wore off overseas. Of course, what really happened was that the pound grew ever weaker over the following two years. Every time we transferred funds to France, while leaving a good proportion behind to, er, recover its value in the imminent future, we lost more and more money in real terms as the building work became far more expensive than we could have possibly foreseen.

And so, as we drove into Gréolières to begin our new life in France on the third of May, the settlement of Ron's case in just a month's time was beginning to take on a significance that we had not previously envisaged. We had supported Ron, as would anyone a close friend in their hour of need, with no guarantee of reimbursement: it was the exposure of the quasi-illegal profit-making by the fat cats at a scale beyond words that we were working towards.

But it was now also going to be useful if we could, to some extent, be repaid.

Chapter 7

The village-centre apartment we had secured as home for the duration of the building work was on the top floor of an unwieldy and cumbersome agglomeration of medieval buildings overlooking the village square and, thank goodness, situated directly opposite the bar.

It was reached by five staircases of varying length, width and difficulty of ascendance, so that the installation of even two car loads of possessions took a whole day. Being the "penthouse suite", it allowed us at least the benefit of a small, triangular-shaped terrace, from which we could see the grey walls of the building opposite and a miniscule portion of the mountain on the other side of the valley, but the luxury factor ended at that point.

I had laughed when first entering the premises a few weeks earlier, in my frantic search for accommodation following Gary's foreboding news; there being the choice of two suitable apartments to let in the village. This one had been described to me as having three bedrooms; a requirement made necessary by the fact that Karen's eleven-year-old daughter, Francesca, was fast reaching the point at which her two-year-old sister had long since finished being cute and had become the embodiment of all that pre-pubescent teenagers cannot possibly tolerate in their close proximity, let alone their bedroom.

Three bedrooms! It was basically a vast attic space that had, at some time, been vaguely converted into a family apartment by someone with the constructional skills of a learning-deficient wombat. Various levels were connected by small wooden ladders, and unattached ones at that. There were no barriers to prevent children (or drunk adults) from meeting an untimely death by dropping from the "mezzanine" decking on to the ceramic flooring beneath. The open fireplace, attractive at first, filled the apartment with billowing clouds of smoke at every attempt to make use of its supposed twofold benefit: the central heating and the supply of hot water. The roof leaked in four places every time it rained, the three bedrooms turned out to be different corners of the same room, and exposed, colourful wiring throughout resembled something rendered by an energetic Jackson Pollock. On speed.

We were given a month in which to decide whether to sign a contract for the following year, and were absolutely astonished, coming from Britain, that a place as unfinished, scruffy and downright rustic as this could possibly find its way on to the market.

There were dangerous drops, beautifully exposed stonework, no privacy, stunning wood infrastructures, lethal electrics, a wonderfully quaint kitchen, wasps' nests in the rooflights and a small but breathtaking view of the mountains. We signed without hesitation.

And during those first few weeks, the years of dreaming, visualisation and planning started to become a reality as our mountain wilderness, three hundred metres up the road, underwent the initial stages of its metamorphosis into the home of our future.

As the third member of the team, Gary had enlisted a tall, swarthy and fit chap named Barry. Barry's family history was astonishing. He was the son of an English mother and a Lebanese father, who himself was actually of Palestinian origin – and Jewish at that. Barry had been well-educated and had an oversight of world affairs befitting someone of such cosmopolitan roots. He spoke five languages, including Japanese. The first few days on site were punctuated by an endless stream of political and satirical anecdotes: we shared a common cynicism when it came to the real driving forces behind the charades played out by the world's leaders. I looked forward to working with him.

Soon after we had become established in the village, Gary accompanied me to the nearest, vast, builders' merchant, where we set up an account so that the numerous deliveries of materials to the site would be able to take place without the constant problem of individual, small payments. They were to issue a monthly bill, for which a cheque could be written at the time or thereabouts.

Strangely, Gary asked that I put the account in my name, even though he was to be the builder in charge, as, he said, it would be cheaper in the long run. Whether or not that was the case was beside the point, as subsequent events exposed me as the biggest fool since the gingerbread man thought it might be a good idea to cross a river on the back of a hungry fox.

He also told me that it was standard practice in France for the client to buy all the tools, protective clothing, boots and other necessary secondary items involved with the building process. Trusting, as ever, in the belief that others will be fair with me if I am honourable in my dealings with them, we spent money like water, not for one second thinking it somewhat bizarre that a building business should have income on the one hand, and virtually no expenses whatsoever on the other.

The first couple of weeks also saw the arrival of our *terrassier*, Tony, from Grasse, whose job it would be to create the various terraced levels on which the house could be built. Tony was impressive to watch. Sitting at the controls of his huge, mechanical shovel, he skilfully moved the various levers and knobs with such dexterity that he managed to actually create the impression that the machine was dancing.

After two weeks of monumental effort, the huge terraces finally became clear, flat levels, and massive boulders of more than a metre in diameter were daintily moved about to fill a gap here or provide a retaining wall there, as if they were nothing more than chess pieces on a board. Tony was a grandmaster; this was his endgame.

Nearing the completion of the terracing, Tony arrived one day with a smaller machine mounted on rubber caterpillar tracks to put the finishing touches to his performance. I was just commenting on how well it all seemed to be going so far when a huge jet of water shot vertically into the air from somewhere beneath the digger. A manic few minutes ensued, during which the cause was discovered: Tony had run over the mains supply to our nearest neighbours, as it had not been buried to a sufficient depth. A stopcock was wildly searched for and located, and a solution proposed, when a bemused neighbour emerged, asking if we had any idea as to why the water seemed to have just been cut off. Having explained the problem, I was despatched to our nearest DIY shop to buy a suitable connector, while Gary cleaned up the now ragged ends of the plastic pipe.

That first foray into the world of shopping for materials provided me with a foresight into the potential pitfalls that lay ahead along the long road towards the distant goal of house completion. Back in England, I would have popped down the road to any one of six DIY megastores in the vicinity, which were fully stocked and always open; even on a Sunday. But here, it was to be oh, so different.

The drive down to Grasse or Vence took about three quarters of an hour, although the near absence of other road users and the inspiring scenery always made the journey pleasurable. However, the realisation that we needed something we had failed to order earlier normally took place towards late morning, leading to the unexpected result that one would arrive at the store just as they were closing for lunch. Even though we already knew that time stands still for the French at midday, allowing for respectful two-hour worship at the altar of the dining table, it was going to be a long time before we could plan our days with any sense of logical time management.

And so there I would be, having driven down from the hills for the best part of an hour, faced with nothing to do for a further two hours until the doors of acquisition reopened before me. What is one to do at a time like this? It wasn't worth driving back and returning again, for that would absorb the same amount of my day as if I just waited somewhere convenient. Of course, the only places that are open at midday are the restaurants and bars, and trips such as these would see me waltzing back into the appropriate store at two o'clock in the afternoon, fatter and in a far jollier state of mind than before.

Until, that is, within two minutes of entering the place, when I'd be told that what I had come for was out of stock until the next week.

At this point, as the day was written off completely, I'd resort to another drink to calm the nervous twitching that had set itself up in my left eyelid.

Back on site, Tony had virtually completed his work; the final problem being the presence of a huge mass of solid rock projecting into one corner of the foundations-to-be, and on which even the might of his largest machine was unable to make any impression. He decided that we would have to call in a friend of his – a friend skilled in the art of sticking large sticks of dynamite into rocks and blowing them to pieces. This sounded exciting, but added a new and unforeseen additional cost to the project.

The friend turned up a couple of days later, sporting a lopsided hat, a broad smile and a vanful of the most dangerous-looking equipment I could possibly have imagined. Electrical cables of varying lengths and gauges, detonating devices, huge power drills and open boxes of what appeared to be fat, brightly-coloured candles vied for space in what had once been a small, black trades van, but what now looked like a rejected vehicle from the set of Mad Max, with a manically grinning driver of equally theatrical appearance. I hoped he knew what he was doing.

An hour later, everyone on site, including Karen, who had come up from the apartment to watch the pyrotechnics, was given a two-minute warning in advance of the detonation. Having drilled numerous holes into the rock and packed them full of explosives, our friend now stood some fifty metres off to one side. He was connected to his handiwork by a thick cable carrying the unseen power which was hopefully going to blow the offending presence to smithereens. We clapped our hands over our ears, tried not to close our eyes in abject terror so that we would actually see the explosion and have something to tell our grandchildren, and counted down the last few seconds before ignition. The man pressed the detonator. Our hearts missed an expectant beat …

And the rock quietly went "ploof", cracking but not moving, as a wispy column of dust gently rose into the air. And that was it. I attempted, I think unsuccessfully, judging by the smirk on Gary's face, to absolutely not give the impression that I had been expecting something a little more dramatic, as we went over to watch Tony remove the rocky fragments with his machine.

Chapter 8

With the mountainside now bearing the scars of terracing, the next job, along with digging the trenches for the foundations, was to find a crane to hire or buy. With the entrance lane from the road being some fifteen metres higher than the level on which the foundations were to be laid, we were going to require some mechanical help to shift delivered materials down on to the terraces below.

Gary successfully located a second-hand electric crane for sale that appeared to suit our needs; the only drawback being that it was situated some sixty kilometres distant, not far from Draguignan in the Var. So, one fine day, during the period in which the Panther was still covered by British insurance, Gary and I dropped the hood and started out on a pleasant drive into the next county, or *département*, passing through Grasse en route.

As we drove through the town's medieval streets, I was reminded of the novel *Perfume*, by Patrick Suskind. The story is a bizarre foray into the surreal world of the senses, and Grasse is the city of destination for the strange and macabre protagonist, Grenouille.

Grasse was, and still is to this day, the perfume capital of the world. The various scent manufacturers use the wild lavender, orange blossom and a myriad of other beautiful floral species from the hills and valleys around the city to create the base oils from which perfumes are developed by world-renowned scent-houses.

As Grenouille surveys the city for the first time, he is struck by the filth of the cramped streets, some no more than a metre wide, through which flows the effluent from many sources, and I, too, was amazed by the complexity and darkness of the old town. It seems paradoxical that a city famed for its production of world-class perfumes is also the grubbiest, gloomiest place in the vicinity.

However, although it still seems as though the medieval quarter is pervaded by an almost foreboding sense of decay, the current city-wide refurbishment programmes are adding new colour and light to this wonderfully absorbing, time-drenched metropolis.

As we drove into the Var, west of Grasse, the strikingly different landscape of red, rocky outcrops and scrubby green forests once again greeted my eyes. The somewhat other-worldly impression one gets of this region is reinforced by sudden patches of bare, blackened skeletons of trees and shrubs, ravaged by the ubiquitous forest fires that seem to occur with ever-increasing frequency with each passing summer. Set against the electric blue of the all-encompassing sky, the searing sharpness of all one perceives is almost overwhelming.

We found the crane, neatly folded and parked beside the road outside a rambling, open-air assortment of ageing building equipment. The owner arrived a little later and we settled his bill. He then hitched the old machine up to his truck and, with Gary and me now back in the car, we set off at a rather slower pace than that with which we had arrived. There had been a slight disagreement over the choice of route back to Gréolières. Gary had wanted to return via Grasse, as it seemed the most obvious and quickest passage. For some reason, however, the owner had insisted on taking a small, snaking road, which led up into the mountains to the north, then back east towards the Wolf Valley beyond and on, ultimately, to Gréolières.

The reason was to become very clear after about thirty minutes of slow progress through the steep and sinuous streets of the small villages which lay along the awkward itinerary that the chap had chosen. As we crawled, almost vertically at times, it seemed, out of yet another beautiful hilltop village into the forests beyond, the crane swaying dangerously from side to side and almost taking the legs off an unsuspecting village grandmother, we approached a log cabin among the trees to the left of the road, and the driver ahead slowed to a halt.

'What the fuck's he doin' now?' shouted a very tetchy Gary, whose idea of coming to help me with the purchase of the crane had not involved an extra two-hour voyage of unbelievable distance into the wild and savage hinterland in which we now found ourselves. It was like needing a pint of milk from the corner shop, and being told that a trip through the Australian outback, the forests of Brazil, and the Glaswegian Gorbals on the way back would seem like a sensible route to follow.

The answer to Gary's eloquently phrased question soon became apparent, along with the reason for the bizarre choice of route. As we looked on from the car behind, the driver descended from his truck, slammed the door, and wandered towards the little house in the woods. Running towards him with open arms was a woman, and they were soon hugging, then necking, in wild oblivion of the stunned onlookers in the parked car. We had been led on this ridiculous goose chase so that the man could spend five minutes in the arms of his lover! Gary seethed. I laughed, and began to fall in love myself, with the optimistic opportunism that I was beginning to feel existed and throbbed throughout the very fabric of this, our strange and colourful new world.

A few minutes later, as we continued on our way along a particularly lonely and densely-forested lane, it appeared that all was not well with the crane ahead. Its weaving suddenly became terrifyingly three-dimensional, and Gary quickly noticed the cause: the right-hand tyre was unravelling, resembling a Catherine wheel in its death-throes as strips and rags of radial rubber threw themselves, with ever-increasing velocity, into the road around them.

We flashed our lights. We honked our horn. We waved our arms.

We shouted, and eventually found ourselves screaming, in a desperate attempt to get the driver to arrest his dangerous and insistent onward progress. All to no avail. Whatever had passed between him and his girlie ten minutes earlier had obviously floated his boat to such wonderful extent that he was now totally oblivious of any connection with reality or, it seemed, the road beneath. His ability to detect the violent lurchings of a twelve-metre crane at the rear, which was now jumping around on two tyres, one of which was fast-resembling a huge spinning plate of regurgitated black spaghetti, was rendered absolutely null and void.

He came to a halt only when the expanding mess finally exploded from the wheel rim with sufficient volume to shake him from his romantic reverie, the crane finally rolling on to its side, as its metal girders creaked a thankful sigh of rusty relief.

A hurried debate was held there at the roadside and the seller agreed to bring the crane, complete with new tyre, to the site the following day. I doubted it myself, since the actual location of the incident and the exceedingly corroded state of the huge wheel-nuts suggested to me that we would be waiting for some time to come. I was amazed, therefore, and also hugely relieved when the chap arrived in Gréolières the very next day, slowly towing the machine behind him, complete with repaired tyre in place. The other one, however, looked as if it may go the same way as its partner at any point, or as soon as I attempted to repeat the sale myself at the end of the building work.

That was some way off though, and for now we occupied ourselves with attempting to move the crane from the roadside where it had been left, down the steep and rough incline which was currently serving as our site entrance, and into place on the first of the terraced levels below. This was to be achieved with the help of Tony, who would lower the folded crane down the drive ahead of his large caterpillar-tracked digger. Connecting the two machines was a three-inch wide, worn, woven strap, which looked to me as if it would barely restrain a yapping Yorkshire terrier.

I made my doubts audible, but Gary assured me that it was well up to the job. He was just explaining to me that it had been used for doing the same sort of thing countless times before, when the strap, now as taut as a tightrope, suddenly snapped apart and five tonnes of folded steel crane began to trundle off down the incline. Four thousand euros and several days of acquisition were looking completely wasted when, incredibly, just as the rolling mass started to gather momentum, a well-placed rock turned the crane, and it gently tipped over the edge of the first terrace and came to a rest, albeit a little unevenly, in almost exactly the place we had planned for it.

Half an hour was sufficient for Tony to nudge it into its final operating position and, not wanting to tempt fate any further that day, we hastily despatched to the village bar and sank a few beers in celebration of the installation of our primary power tool.

Chapter 9

The next day, Gary and I marked out the lines for the foundations with white-powdered chalk, following which Tony returned to dig the trenches as the next stage in preparation for the actual construction of the house.

It soon became clear, however, that apart from a few metres in one corner, the entire fourteen-metre square "footprint" of the house was positioned over a solid bed of rock, rendering Tony's attempts at trench-digging not only impossible, but unneccessary. So, after spending a week with brooms, rakes and pickaxes, clearing the loose debris from the rocky surfaces and overlaying this with a complex steel reinforcing system, we were ready to order several lorry-loads of pre-mixed concrete. This would be poured into the shallow trenches, forming the foundations and the floor of the basement in one fell swoop.

It was during the preparation of the foundations that I saw my first sizeable snake. I was sweeping clean a trench for a wall which would be partially underground, with the huge facade of excavated mountain rock rising six metres above me on either side. Suddenly, a slimy black head shot out of the rock face, looked left and right, and slithered several metres horizontally along a rocky ledge before finding another cleft into which it disappeared without trace. It had been well over a metre long and about four or five centimetres in diameter, and I had been truly startled by its abrupt appearance. It impressed upon me the fact that we had probably disturbed many creatures' habitats with our violent and noisy invasion into this wilderness, and I must admit I felt a little guilty at our small contribution to the global scarring of nature by the insidious spread and development of the human species.

It was now early June, and the forests and meadows surrounding the site were a dazzling display of verdant colour. The grass was lush and green, thriving on the rains from occasional early summer storms, and the hillsides shouted a technicolour riot of wild floral brilliance. And, as late springtime heralded fertile abundance all around us, we made plans for the return trip to England for the birth of our new baby.

Since Karen was now over eight months pregnant, we were to make the long trek north this time by train. We had contacted various friends back in Norwich and had managed to find a house in which to stay for ten days, while the owners holidayed in the Lake District.

The baby was due at the beginning of July, so we packed our bags and headed for Nice railway station in the heat of mid-June, Barry kindly giving us a lift down in order to save expenses on car parking while we were away.

Emily was in high spirits as we arrived at the station, excited by the prospect of travelling by train for the first time that she could remember, and chattered away uncontrollably at the sight of so many people coming and going from all over the continent.

We boarded the TGV (*Train de Grande Vitesse*), and settled down to enjoy a journey that would take just six hours to reach England, before slowing considerably as the train tickety-tacked its way along an old, badly maintained line on the other side of the Channel Tunnel. On the French side, the train was a revelation. Travelling at three hundred kilometres per hour, it felt as if we were flying in a low-level aircraft, as we sped on our way to Lille, through the ever-changing countryside that we had driven through just six weeks earlier. And then, emerging into the grey of a rainy day at Folkestone, we slowed to a snail's pace as we headed towards London on a line of seemingly stone-age quality.

How on earth, I thought at the time, could France have managed to build the link from the tunnel to the receiving terminals at Paris and Lille at, logically, more or less the same time as the tunnel itself had been built, while, seven years later, the various privatised interests in England were still bickering over the financing of the link at the other end? Oh, the glory of privatisation! Maximum profit, minimum costs and therefore minimum maintenance has to be the prime consideration of these capitalist industrialists. Several horrific accidents on British railways in recent years are a further, and far more terrifying, result of the madness that is endemic in our money-hungry society. When, I wonder in constant amazement, will people's lives be more important than profit?

Chapter 9

Arriving at Norwich station at nine o'clock in the evening, we were met by another kind friend, who had offered to transport the three of us to our borrowed lodgings in the city. We collapsed into bed, and three days later, Karen was admitted for what turned out to be the most difficult and protracted labour I had ever witnessed. Over the next two days, with a succession of false alarms, the tension rose as our twofold expectations drew towards their fulfilment.

And so it came to be that, on the gloomy evening of June the twenty-ninth, I was at the house with Emily and Julie, our babysitter, when Ron, bringing what could only be good news, arrived at the door. But, from the moment he entered the dark hallway, the hairs rose forebodingly along the length of my neck.

There was something wrong.

Horribly, sickeningly, wrong.

Chapter 10

After two and a half years, the agony of expectation made it difficult to contain the plethora of questions battling to pass my lips at what was, for us, a singularly momentous point in time.

Trembling, I invited Ron in, made some tea and endeavoured to make small talk in the nervous and jittery fashion that accompanies occasions of such magnitude. Fifteen taut and tension-charged minutes later, we left Emily, and also Francesca, who had rejoined us a little earlier from her stay in Tenerife, with Julie and made our way to the only environment that could ameliorate the apprehension in the air: the pub of closest proximity.

Installed at the bar, with pints in place, Ron looked me straight in the eyes with an iron-hard expression, which could only mean, in its rigid seriousness, the outcome we had always known to be possible but had not dared contemplate.

'So,' I said, voice quavering, 'they've reached a settlement?'

'Listen, my friend,' Ron replied, 'I have a tale to tell that would shock the world; a story of deeds so foul in their criminal corruption that few would believe what I am about to tell you.'

My stomach and intestines wrestled in their attempt to be the first to drop from my quivering rectum, so I gave them something else to do, pulling long and hard on my beer.

'I duly toddled off to London today,' Ron began, 'as I'd received a call from my lawyers, informing me that they'd finally received an offer from the fast-food chain that was acceptable to them, and sufficient to obviate proceedings in the High Court tomorrow. I, as much as your dear self, my friend, wanted nothing more than to see those bastards exposed for all their filthy corruption. But, as my London law-firm had offered, uniquely, to fight this on a "No Win, No Fee" basis, it's always been their prerogative to accept a deal if it satisfied the interests of their establishment and their client. I therefore set off for London with reasonable expectations of a decent settlement for all of us.

'My friend, I cannot convey to you the dread I felt as I entered the room and observed the company present. The partner who had taken my case on, and who himself had proclaimed a hatred of dirty deeds by the world's largest corporate interests, was sitting, head bowed, in a far corner of a long table, presided over by a new, and unbeknown to me, helmsman. What could only be representatives from Satan's own syndicate, the fast-food bastards, made up the other members of the assembled party, along with what appeared to be a female secretary or recorder of some sort.

As I took my place at the table, desperately trying to catch the eye of the now superseded partner, whose long face gazed fixedly at the floor, I was informed that a settlement had been agreed; meaning that we had won. Their eight hundred and fifty thousand-odd pounds legal bill would be paid for by the fast-food chain, so I had no expenses to worry about as agreed. Good result for the lawyers, eh?

I asked them how much they had seen as a fitting sum to accept on my behalf. A sum which would go some way to recompensing me for the theft of years of hard work, the loss of a worldwide income for nearly three years, the torment my family had endured and the mental anguish I had personally undergone while these commercial criminals had wrecked my life.

'One hundred thousand pounds,' was the bastard's unbelievable reply!

'My mouth dropped open, Ben. I was in shock ... staggered. After several seconds, when I finally managed to move my jaw again, my friend, I explained, although they well knew, that I wouldn't see a penny of such a paltry sum, as my creditors would swallow that and lots more, before I could benefit myself.

' "B ... but," and now I was spitting at him, Ben, I really was, "but we were suing for a sum which you agreed would be in the seven-figure range! Even the newspapers printed that! That's absolutely fuck all, you know it, and what's more, these bloody bastards will get away with no court exposure, no bad publicity whatsoever, in exchange for that! But why? Why are we not going to court for a proper settlement and the justice you know I deserve ... *why*?"

'And then words which chilled me like no others I had ever heard were directed at me by the new, stony-faced chairman, who sat opposite. He simply said, and I quote word for horrible word:

' "We have decided after all that we do not want to ..."'

Ron, lips trembling, took a pull on his beer and tried again.

' "We have decided after all that we do not want to embarrass the Americans in the High Court tomorrow."'

Those words will haunt me for life. Even at the highest levels of the English legal system, it seemed, here was proof that none of the contemptible, ignominious individuals who are installed to protect the ordinary citizen and work for their best interests, are immune to the obscene offers that come their way in the form of sullied sheaves of notes in grubby brown envelopes.

And there it was.

'Well,' I said to Ron, manically laughing as I saw fifty thousand pounds of our own capital float gently away on a tide of filth, 'it's only money!' and, trembling, I ordered two more beers.

Chapter 11

Strangely, the following day dawned bright and clear, and I made ready to welcome home the wonderful couple who had been so generous to accommodate us in our hour of need.

I was also called back to the hospital for the final moments of a harrowing two-day ordeal for Karen. After forty-eight hours of a stop-start labour, Thomas James eventually decided to make his presence felt in the early hours of the first of July. And, still finding himself in mischievous mood, continued the anguish by developing jaundice, necessitating a further few days in hospital for his poor mother.

Simultaneously, since the house we had used to this point was no longer available, we moved the rest of the family across the city, to lodge with some more unusually helpful friends while Karen recovered. I took little Emily with me to the home of Diana Parsons – an outrageously fit eighty-six-year-old friend of the family – while, to share the load, Francesca was put up by Diana's daughter Emily (no coincidence) and her partner Steve, and we all awaited the homecoming of Karen and Thomas.

I had first met Diana and her late husband, Ewart – a veteran of the Canadian Air Force – about ten years previously, at which time I had been running my first gallery in a small courtyard in the heart of Norwich. I had just separated from my first wife and, being in need of some cheering up, had been invited to Diana and Ewart's annual house party in early January. A smashingly well-timed event, I thought to myself, as I walked up to the welcoming Edwardian city-mews house, the sound of happy conversation and the warm glow of numerous lamps of all shapes and sizes streaming from within. As soon as my feet crossed the threshold, a large wine glass was pressed into my hand by Steve and was promptly filled to the brim with a rich, mellow red. I somehow knew that I was going to enjoy the company of these people.

The house was crammed fully wall-to-wall with an astonishingly animated and diverse miscellany of the most interesting folk I had ever had the pleasure, and good fortune, to meet. Members of Parliament rubbed shoulders with artists, and ageing gentlemen sporting tweeds and handlebar moustaches flirted with young, eccentrically-garbed students. (Diana and Ewart had enjoyed a long and active history in campaigning for the Labour Party; that is, in the days before it became more right-wing than a Bible-thumping Texan.) The whole occasion was lubricated by copious volumes of delicious red wine, or maybe after the first six glasses the quality deteriorated, but if so, no-one was in a position to notice.

At the end of the evening, the final stragglers and best friends were privileged to be entertained at the table by the family, Diana and her daughter Emily having whipped up something exotic in the kitchen during the previous hour or two. Laden with garlic and olive oil, the food evoked the warmth and radiance of Provence, and planted the first seeds in my soul that were to bear such life-enriching fruit some ten years later. At this point in the evening, Diana, having quaffed probably more wine than anyone else present, entertained us with anecdotes from her exotically-packed past.

Sporting blonde, straight hair cut into an asymmetrical bob, and being always sharply yet artistically attired, Diana often looked like the quintessential twenties' flapper girl, and she still laughed and frolicked her way through life with the energy of a woman half her age.

Now, with Ewart having sadly passed away, I felt privileged to have been invited to stay in her cosy home, the walls of which were covered from floor to ceiling by her beautiful watercolours of the people and places so dear to her heart. These would now play host to the noisy intrusion of an energetic three-year-old, a new-born baby, a bedraggled and exhausted mother and, trying to hold it all together while the French dream began to collapse around our feet, a very depressed me.

In the wake of Ron's dark tidings, I was not coping at all well by this point, and it must be said that Karen did an amazing job of trying to keep our spirits up; taking care of a newborn baby in a strange and cramped environment and diplomatically managing the imposition of such mayhem into an elderly lady's private surroundings.

Chapter 11

A further talk with Gary over the telephone from France only served to deepen the depression that I now retrospectively realise was threatening to engulf me. Due to difficulties with the terrain and slope of the mountain, it was going to be necessary to create, in effect, a whole three metres of supporting structure beneath the house. This would be needed in order to bridge the vertical gap between the flat and solid base that we had created, and the ground level of the structure as required by the authorities, in order that the roof should be at the correct finished height in reference to the mountain when completed.

On top of the huge losses suffered by the seemingly devious actions of the American chain, we were also losing money in real terms daily, as the euro continued to strengthen against the pound.

We dithered about the transferral of our funds, being distracted from any thoughts of financial planning by the difficult birth of our latest addition and the very necessary subsequent attention to mother and baby. And now it looked as though it was going to be even more expensive to complete the French house than previously envisaged, due to these new technical problems just communicated to me.

As Karen slowly recovered over the next few days and I attempted to prevent a boisterous little girl from causing too much disturbance in Diana's small house, I descended into a whirlpool of mental anguish: I imagined remaining in England, to be housed in a local-authority stop-gap home, while the weeds of despair grew thick and fast across the foundations of our dreams on a beautiful French mountainside.

I started to drink. Heavily. I was lost, beaten, having never been one to give up the fight before. What were we to do? We were going to need at least another hundred and fifty thousand euros on top of the initial funding we had thought would cover the job. Or leave the land, complete with foundations, and return to England. To what?

Finally, seeing defeat rear its ugly head over our horizon, Karen, for the first time in the eight years that I had known her, decided to ring her father for help. Proud Karen, who would never let her parents know when she was in a fix, was resorting to something I know her independent spirit despised. Gerry was cautious. Although we had planned the project meticulously for several years, buying and selling houses and businesses to raise the finance that should have been sufficient, researching the area thoroughly and planning an enterprise based on sound knowledge of the region, as well as studying the language and getting to know the locals, it now appeared that we had been careless. He demurred for a few days, then finally agreed to help us. He kindly arranged a loan of fifty thousand Euros, drawn up legally to avoid any misunderstandings, under extremely generous conditions. We were ecstatic. It is impossible to express the relief we felt. We were going to have to sort something else out in a few months, but at least we could get on with what we had started, and have a little space in which to breathe while we looked for the next source of funds.

Having recently drowned myself in wine to escape the frightening possibility of eventual disappointment, we now cracked open a few more bottles in celebration of the project's continuation.

An insidious drug is alcohol, I've often thought. One drinks at times of unhappiness in an attempt to soften the harshness of reality, one drinks at times of happiness in a celebration of life and, in the absence of either, one drinks because one is bored. Ho hum.

All in all, we spent five weeks in Norwich, in different friends' homes, tents and other spaces, being tolerated by some, and spoilt rotten by others. It was also necessary, of course, to get a passport for little Tom, and I spent a confusing and claustrophobic time in a London passport office in the heat of July to secure the document which would facilitate his passage out of the country. It occurred to me somewhat ridiculous that this tiny, indistinguishable photograph of an anonymous-looking baby of a few days old would be acceptable until he was five years of age, when every passport official would look at the child, then the passport, and break out into a huge smile.

There was now about as much similarity, for example, between Emily and the image in her passport as between the Mona Lisa and a baboon's bottom.

Stresses diverse were beginning to take their toll as we drew towards the day of leaving. Our good friends Margaret and Roy, the final couple to suffer the pleasure of our company, saw us off at the station, waving frantically in what could only have been unrestrained relief at our departure.

Chapter 11

London, Paris, the south. As the train flew towards our destination, an unspoken calmness seemed to descend once more upon the family, and the sight of the stars that shone from the sunny mountainsides inspired new belief in us that we were really going home.

Chapter 12

Barry had kindly offered to meet us in Nice, and did well to squeeze a rather larger family into his small BMW saloon than the one he had dropped off five weeks earlier. As we sped along the Promenade des Anglais, the warmth of the evening, the bright lights of the city and the moon's reflection across the Bay of Angels all helped to reinforce our conviction that emigrating to this beautiful part of the world had been a wise move.

An hour later, as the family tumbled out of the car outside our village apartment, we were enthusiastically welcomed home by Philippe, the bald, goatee-bearded chef from the village pizzeria La Barricade. He was sitting in the square having a late drink with some friends, Thierry and Lyn, to whom we were briefly introduced.

They had just taken on a new lease at the little Provençal restaurant situated on the ground floor of the building in which we were living at the time; they would prove to become very special friends in the weeks and months ahead.

The next morning I needed a break after our long train journey, so I informed Gary that I would see him the following day on site.

We decided to celebrate Tom's birth with a meal at La Barricade early that evening. As we climbed the incline from the village centre to the doors of the restaurant, we were pleasantly surprised to see a blackboard, which had been propped up outside the door, on which was chalked, in large letters: "Bienvenue à petit Thomas." What a fantastic place this was! After just a couple of months, we had been made to feel extraordinarily welcome in this small village, and I found myself filling up at this new manifestation of the geniality of these people. It was also another indication of the extremely different attitudes towards children taken by the French as opposed to their English counterparts.

As we entered the restaurant, Philippe's mother, Jo, rushed up to greet us with the customary kiss on each cheek and immediately asked to hold the new baby. And it was not just the women with this tendency to go soft over babies and small children in general. We were stunned over the following few weeks as all and sundry approached us in the streets of the village to take little Thomas in their arms. Everyone in this place, it seemed, had a natural and uninhibited desire to share in the joy of new birth; even strapping late-teenage boys bedecked in shell suits and gold chains wanted to cuddle the new arrival, along with grandmothers, grandfathers and other children of all ages. This was such a refreshing change from the English experience and, to me at least, a wonderfully normal interaction in a community of human beings. It was a far cry from the society we had left behind, in which often, when announcing a pregnancy, one is greeted with the words: "Oh dear. Another one? What on earth are you going to do?" or other such negative responses. Here, in our cosy French village, the children are celebrated and welcomed with open arms by all and, as a result, generation gaps are virtually unheard of.

I have found this to be generally true of Mediterranean regions, although it was seemingly even more apparent in our own mountain-perched commune. I was offered an amusing explanation for this happy state of affairs as I chatted with an old lady one morning in the village *épicerie*. Following my complimentary comments on the nature in which children were accepted into each others' homes freely, she remarked, with a wry smile on her face:

'Ah! What you have to understand, monsieur, is that the village was different before the tourists and the paragliding.'

'In what way?' I asked, curious.

'Well, up to about fifteen years ago, monsieur, the place was virtually unheard of. This was a small, rural community, which had few dealings with the outside world.'

'Go on,' I said. This was becoming interesting.

'Well, you see, people didn't mix much with those from other parts. Therefore, hmm, this is a little difficult to explain, monsieur. Mmm, well, you know that you see people feeding other people's children and making them welcome in their own homes, and so on?'

'Yes,' I replied, 'their friendliness is remarkable.'

She laughed. 'Yes, but, as I said, the village was quite closed before. No one knew exactly to whom the children belonged! They could even have been yours, so, just in case, you had better feed and look after them all!'

This was hilarious, but I was assured had a grain of truth within.

For whatever reason, however, it was truly a socially amicable place to be.

As we sat in the restaurant that evening, having been greeted by all present, Emily asked if she could go and stroke a friendly-looking dog lying by its master's feet at the next table. I asked the owner if it was safe to do so and, having reassured me it was, he took Emily by the hand and introduced her to his pet. Then, smiling broadly, he took her on his lap and gave her a great hug, telling us what a beautiful little girl she was.

I was again struck by how much more humane this behaviour was when compared with that of the society which we had forsaken, where any communication between children and unknown adults is seen as dangerous or threatening. I was reminded of that hideous phrase used in English schools, "Stranger Danger", by which children are brainwashed into believing that all unknown adults are paedophiles, leading to the situation in which society becomes secularised to such an extent that all normal relationships in the community are lost to a guilty fear of retribution at any close interaction between its members.

Thank you for your contribution to that, Mrs Thatcher. As you said, "There is no such thing as society. There are individual men and women..." Ha! Divide and rule, in other words. It is far easier for any dictator to control his or her people with an iron fist when they have no conception of neighbourhood or loyalty. Once you have convinced people that they have no friends, community or society, they are truly alone, and are therefore powerless to protest with any common strength against unjust decisions made by their government.

On a global scale, too, one witnesses the constant "anti-terrorist" diatribe propaganda from our leaders, the airports overrun with unnecessary numbers of police and members of the military forces.

Of course there are some threats in modern society, but how much simpler it is to get your subjects to implement your schemes for power when they believe they don't have a friend in the world! And how much easier it becomes, when normal interactive human links are destroyed by political propaganda on all sides, to blind the people to one's own terrifying military might, while denouncing the other side for owning a fraction of the quantity of one's own destructive potential. Humbug!

One hears the spurious argument which defends our own massive stockpile of nuclear warheads, while not possibly allowing any Middle-Eastern nation a sniff of the global tinderbox, as they are, let's see, likely to be more extreme in their Islamic fervour. Whereas, on the other hand, it is suggested, we Westerners can be trusted to be sensible, while other nations might actually be stupid enough to press the button.

But which is the only nation on earth ever to have actually pressed the red button of doom? I am sure that the inhabitants of Nagasaki and Hiroshima would have something to say on the matter. Such sickening hypocrisy from the world's most powerful terrorists (the Anglo-American axis) is intolerable. The destruction of the planet by the all-consuming habits and attitudes of the American-led system will have to give way to some sort of environmental common sense, or there will be nothing left for our children and their descendants.

As Fritjof Capra, world-eminent physicist, said in 1975:

> "I believe that the world view implied by modern physics is inconsistent with our present society, which does not reflect the harmonious interrelatedness we observe in nature. To achieve such a state of dynamic balance, a radically different social and economic structure will be needed: a cultural revolution in the true sense of the word. The survival of our whole civilisation may depend on whether we can bring about such a change. It will depend, ultimately, on our ability to adopt some of the yin attitudes of Eastern mysticism; to experience the wholeness of nature and the art of living with it in harmony."

We have always found the pizzas in this part of the world to be of excellent quality, possibly due to the close proximity of Italian tradition (a large part of the Alpes Maritimes actually belonged to Italy right up until the late nineteenth century), but Philippe was an absolute maestro, having been trained by a true Italian master himself. At La Barricade, one was free to devise a personal topping and, knowing that I missed the flavour of a hot curry, he attempted, from time to time, to create something of exceptional piquancy to tantalise my taste buds, grinning mischievously as he threw another handful of chillies across the latest concoction. The children were enthralled when he invited them over to the hole in the wall that served as an oven, their eyes widening at the pile of blazing wood on one side which projected its intense heat across the domed roof of the chamber, to cook to perfection the pizza on the other side.

At the end of our meal that first evening back in Gréolières, we were treated to a complimentary digestif by Philippe's mother, Jo, who, like many others in the region, brewed weird and wonderful liqueurs from whichever fruit happened to be in season at the time. During the summer months, it was raspberries, and the deliciously-flavoured result was dangerously impossible to drink in the small quantities for which it was intended.

With the warming liquid mixing with the wine of earlier, and being surrounded on all sides by open-hearted friendship and acceptance, the problems associated with our financial situation melted gently into the background; it seemed as though nothing could disturb a mutual feeling of peace and security.

The real problems, however, were about to begin.

Chapter 13

The following morning, I was struck by the hugely encouraging sight of the first walls of the new house which had been built during our absence in England. And Gary had come up with an ingenious method of dealing with the constraints of our new financial predicament.

The house was originally to have been constructed on two levels containing accommodation for the family, with the rooms to let having been designed as part of a separate, two-storey building along with a garage. Given the fact that we now had an enormous shortfall in available funds, and that the house had an empty void beneath it as a result of its position on the side of the mountain, Gary had decided to incorporate all the guestrooms on the lowest level of the house. This obviated entirely the need for the separate structure and cleverly used what would otherwise have been a vast, empty, wasted basement space below. He had also planned to modify the size of the family accommodation, by contracting the upper house while maintaining its exact proportions, thereby creating a huge, south-facing terrace facing the valley.

These were brilliant ideas, and I set about the concrete-mixing that day with renewed vigour and a smile on my face. The fact that we were completely deviating from the original plans worried me a little, but further talking with Gary put my mind at rest to some extent. We were, he explained, losing one structure completely, and the authorities could hardly complain about something that involved less intrusion into the hillside. The house would be smaller as well, but the same shape, simply nestling back deeper into the terrain around it. And the walls below would have to be built anyway, to support the house at the correct level above them; the only difference being that we were now about to utilise the volume contained within. All of this sounded more than reasonable, and I put my nagging doubts to one side. We had no choice, anyway: we had to save costs at every turn from here on in. Thank God, I thought, for the apparent lack of staged building regulation control in France.

In England, along with the obvious planning permission that one needs to obtain for any new structure, it is also required that the proposed design meets safety requirements when it comes to the actual building methods used. This leads to time-consuming and costly visits to the site by inspectors who, at regular and specified stages of the work, verify that the construction utilises the correct, adequately-sized components with which the building is being formed. In France, it seems that, having obtained planning consent, the work progresses to completion, and a certificate of conformity is obtained at the finish, there being no interim site visits during the construction process.

This was a potential problem, therefore: that we would never receive such a certificate if we applied for one, due to the many changes that had been made to the original design; and we would thus find it difficult to sell the house if and when required. Never intending to move on from such a beautiful place, however, this did not appear to be a great difficulty; especially having spoken to my architect shortly after, who assured me that he had "friends" in the trade and that a sale could probably be achieved without the need for a certificate of conformity at any time in the future if we so desired!

Yes, it can be said that there is more paperwork in France, and that there are sometimes far more rules and regulations to satisfy in any new project such as this, but the vast majority of the population tend to ignore a large proportion of them, including, it appears from time to time, the authorities.

A rather amusing example of this involved some Australian friends of ours, who had moved into a house in the village of Cipières, situated on the opposite side of the valley from where we were building. With her husband working away on a yacht for a large part of the year, Mandy was left to oversee the refurbishment of the house alone. Being a creative sort of individual, she had come up with all sorts of ideas by which she intended to modernise, in sympathetic fashion, the interior. Having thus made her plans, and knowing nothing of the local requirements and legislation governing what she would or would not be able to do, she decided to make an appointment with the local mayor to establish what would be permitted. She received an amusing response, indicating the laid-back approach to life in this corner of the world.

'Basically,' she was told, 'we don't care what you do with the place as long as you maintain its interior character. For God's sake, though, please don't talk about it too openly with your neighbours until you've made friends with them all, because they might complain to us that you're not sticking to the regulations and then we'd have to get involved ...'

It seems that even those in positions of authority would rather spend long hours over boozy lunches in the village restaurant than actually be put in a position in which they may have to carry out any unnecessary work, as long as everyone was happy. I was beginning to love the Mediterranean approach to life.

The following day on site Gary introduced me to a new member of the team, who had been taken on to assist us with the period of most physically-demanding work about to commence. Paul was a slim, fair, tanned chap of happy disposition and jovial demeanour, whose presence immediately lightened what had started to become, for me at least, a rather unpleasant working atmosphere created by the often negative approach that Gary had taken to the world around him.

He was an Eeyore type of person, who, when addressed with the words "Good morning!", would respond with "Is it?", or if one casually remarked "Lovely day!", in his vicinity, would dismally counter with something along the lines of: "Hmm, but it's going to rain tomorrow". He was constantly critical of, and laughed only at the expense of, others, with a seeming inability to communicate openly and honestly with his acquaintances. This dearth of empathy also led to the rather darker manifestation of his character in the form of continuous verbal abuse, which he felt compelled to use against those around him, along with their work. This was the first house I had ever built, so naturally I looked to him for explanations of techniques or the use of tools with which I was not familiar, my queries often being rewarded with an affected frown, followed by:

"But I just fuckin' told you; don't you fuckin' listen or what?" and other such silver-tongued examples of social interaction.

At first I ignored this constant stream of anger, then became depressed by its daily regularity and, finally, simply felt extremely sorry for this individual who was driven to rubbish everyone and everything in his presence. Something, I surmised, must have damaged him to such an extent in the past that he had a constant need to prove his superiority and validity at all costs, but in an extreme and endlessly aggressive manner. He hated the French. He hated the way they drove, or the way they built. They couldn't be trusted, he said. No one could be trusted. No one, it appeared, was as good as him, he would relentlessly remind us, and it began to get me down.

Barry was an intelligent and educated individual, but, for some reason or other, chose to shadow Gary, reiterating to me everything that Gary had said to me not half an hour earlier, in a failed attempt to force home the notion of his master's omnipotence. If Gary was the insecure, pugnacious playground bully, then Barry was the skinny hanger-on, standing behind his mentor, waving a supporting fist in the air and grimacing at Gary's chosen victim. A bizarre couple indeed.

Strangely, in other areas of life, they both presented as reasonably sociable characters, but away from friends and family, this ridiculous need for verbal truculence manifested itself incessantly. Before we had started working together, Gary had actually warned me that, on site, he would need to be recognised as the boss, but I hadn't realised the full import of his words at the time. Now, I considered laying them off, but at this stage in the building programme I still believed that Gary knew more than others about local construction methods, having seen the marvellous home he had built for himself. I also had no idea where I would begin to source a new builder who would be prepared to carry on with another's work, and, coupled with the ever-present problem of the language, I decided to bite my lip and just get on with it until the job was finished.

Paul, on the other hand, was a breath of fresh air, and we worked together well, sharing among other things a love of the music which had emanated from Liverpool during the post-punk era. On one occasion, I was pushing a heavy barrow laden with concrete along some board or other when Paul suddenly shouted across:

'Hey! Remember *Villiers Terrace* by the Bunnymen? What a classic sound they created back then!'

'Bloody hell!' I retorted, 'I'd completely forgotten that one! I'm sure I've got it at home. Pop over later and we'll have a drink and play some of those old tracks. Oh, and what about *Over the Wall*? Brilliant, cutting stuff!'

'Fuckin' pile o' shit, Echo and the Bunnymen.' This was Gary.

'Yeah, pile o' shit.' Barry.

Paul and I simply smiled at each other, shaking our heads, and continued working.

As summer turned into autumn, and the mountainsides became mottled with an ever-changing mantle of earthy colour, there were moments of real beauty supplied by our surroundings, alleviating the depressing atmosphere created by the humans we were forced to spend our time with.

One fine morning, I was the first on site and, just as I was walking around the corner of a wall to collect a tool from the uncompleted room within, I was met by the stare of a mighty stag, whose lofty gaze met mine in shocked silence. I had never seen one of these creatures at such close quarters before, and his air of supremacy was something to behold. I stepped back slowly, and he carefully picked his way past me and out into the forest encircling the house. On making enquiries in the village, I was told that we were building right in the middle of his territory, and I again felt the pangs of guilt at what we were doing to the immediate environment.

However, I am pleased to say that, to this very day, he still patrols his domain around our home, thankfully having accepted this brutal invasion on to his terrain, and can be seen regularly as the sun sets in the west, his noble head silhouetted against the sky, in a grassy clearing just a hundred metres from our terrace.

Chapter 14

As the summer progressed to its conclusion beneath a dazzling display of blue and gold, we became overwhelmed by an intimidating quantity of administrative and family-related difficulties.

I enquired as to our status regarding health care and was advised to keep, although not technically permissible without an English address, the "E111" form, which I had brought with us from England, until we actually started the letting business. Since I was fully occupied with building the house, it was impossible to take on a paid job and thereby make insurance contributions, and thus we were unable to become covered by the French system at that point.

Another item of importance which needed sorting out was schooling for the children. We had visited the village school during a previous reconnaissance trip and were informed that Emily, then three, would be welcome to attend as and when she and we felt comfortable; the only stipulation being that all children attending the school should be "clean" – in other words no longer wearing nappies during the daytime. I asked what the nursery fees would be and was struck dumb by the answer: there were none! This was wonderful. She was welcome to attend the *Maternelle* section of the school for a few mornings, or full days, or whatever suited us as a family, until the time came for her to start full-time at six years of age.

The first days were, admittedly, difficult. The poor girl had only begun to talk at all just a year earlier, and here she was being thrown into a foreign environment with no previous knowledge of the language. However, following a period of no more than a month, she became eager each morning to go to school, and was making firm friends among the other children in the village. It was astounding to hear the perfect French accent that accompanied every new word she learned and within a few months she was bilingual and learning both languages in perfect tandem.

Schooling for Francesca, however, proved to be quite a different matter. We had made enquiries as to which school she should attend at the age of eleven, the age when most children go up from the junior schools to the *collèges* until they are fourteen. We were told that she came under the jurisdiction of the college at Le Rouret, an hour's bus ride from the village. Just before the start of the summer holidays, we had made an appointment to see the head teacher with a view to organising a place for Francesca in the autumn.

On arrival at the school, we had been met by an extremely stern-looking man who, knowing in advance that we were English, asked us bluntly if Francesca was fluent in the French language. I started to explain that of course she was not able to speak the language yet, intending to say that the best way to learn a foreign language is to submerge oneself in it on a daily basis, but I was cut off.

She would not be welcome at the school, the man flatly told us, until she was a fluent French speaker. We left with our tails between our legs, and sought help from other parents in the village.

An angel came our way in the form of Claudine, the amiable, motherly owner of La Vieille Auberge, the village bar/tobacconist in the central square. Claudine was one of those gorgeously smiling, huggable types, in whose presence one is reminded of warm scones and cocoa, summer evenings on the lawn, and a lullaby at bedtime.

She was the cuddly personification of love and laughter, care and capability, authority and affection. She knew everything that happened in the village, helped whenever she could, and seemed to have something constructive to offer on every subject under the sun.

And so it was that, on hearing of our problem at Le Rouret, she defiantly spoke out against him that dared flout his responsibility towards the education of our youth, and offered, then and there, to go and speak with him on our behalf. She told us that he had an absolute obligation to accept all children residing within his catchment area, although he was known to be a staunch conservative, disliking the presence of foreigners in his school. She promptly shut her doors at two in the afternoon, placed a message across the window to the effect that she would be back at four o'clock, and set off on the two-hour return journey to put things straight for us.

Again, we were flabbergasted at not only the willingness that the villagers were demonstrating in their desire to help us, but the fact that here now was someone who was actually sacrificing business in the cause of such assistance, and we watched her departure in silent, awe-stricken appreciation.

Having given the schoolmaster a piece of her mind, she returned with the news that, although he had acquiesced, accepting the fact that he was under an obligation towards Francesca, he thought it might be better if she attended a school in Grasse, which offered a specially-adapted course for foreigners. Here, she would be given intensive lessons in the language, after which she would find it easier to integrate in the high school at Le Rouret the following year.

Claudine had taken a note of the school's location, the teacher to whom we should address our request, and a telephone number with which we could make an appointment to enrol her before the new term. Why on earth the man had not given us this information when we first approached him was beyond us, but at least now, and again thanks to the amazing altruism of the villagers to whom we owed so much, we had managed to surmount another hurdle. From that moment on, I decided, I would spend as much money as was available on beer in Claudine's bar in an effort to repay her magnanimity.

In fact, it was while sitting supping beer outside the bar in the heat of a September Saturday that I received my first piece of social counsel or local knowledge since arriving in the area. Into the square, astride a beautiful chestnut mare, long grey tresses framing his face, a ruddy complexion accentuating his Red Indian features, came Christian. Otherwise known as "Geronimo", he was a horseman from Cipières, on the far side of the valley. My family and I had made the acquaintance of this man in the bar a few days earlier; I had been immediately impressed by his magnetic, affable character.

He dismounted and made his way over to my table in the sun and, as I rose to greet him, he grabbed me by the shoulders and planted a firm kiss on either cheek. I was both touched and honoured; I had heard that only when one is accepted as a close friend does another man kiss one on the cheeks in the traditional way. Taking a seat, he offered to buy me a drink, and we relaxed into the easy banter that is typical of these parts during long summer afternoons.

He informed me that he had worked in southern England for a year at some juncture long past, but his English, rusty at best, became steadily more unintelligible as we drank one, then two more large beers, at which point my rudimentary French must have been equally difficult for him to comprehend. As we commenced our fourth pints, he leaned in towards me as though about to give utterance to words of great moment and, slurring as he spoke, with one finger raised in an indication of warning, said:

'Ben, zere is somesing you must understand to be happy in your life in ze France.'

'Go on,' I replied simply, not wanting to risk the messy mistakes with words that are always probable when one attempts full sentences in a state of near-inebriation.

'When you take ze girlfreends ...' he attempted, before I cut him short.

'B ... but I'm married!' I stuttered. 'You've met my wife!'

'When you take ze girlfreends ...' he tried again, obviously not having understood me, so I interjected once more.

'B ... but, Christian...' and this time it was his turn to stop my flow, as he raised his voice slightly and continued,

'When you take your girlfreends, Ben, all will be well if you remember zat zere weel be no problem if zey are at least from ze next village. Closer zan zat and zere will be ze problems, ok?'

I laughed out loud at this most sensible piece of advice, and the acceptance as normal of all that which is anathema in other parts of the world, and replied:

'And I suppose any man that I see flirting with my wife will also be from the next village, eh?' and we laughed together at the ludicrously amusing village-swapping scenarios which could be played out against a backdrop of such time-honoured tradition.

Christian lived rent-free in a part of a large holiday property in Cipières, in return for which he acted as its caretaker, maintaining the house and its sizeable swimming pool. As we parted company, he informed me that there were no clients in the house that week, and invited our family over for a barbecue and a cooling dip. The following day, therefore, we rolled up *en famille*, to be greeted by an assortment of folk whom Christian had also invited as his poolside guests.

Chapter 14

Stuffed full of barbecued fish from the local river, washed down with seemingly endless quantities of chilled Provençal rosé, I found myself chatting to a chap laid out on a sun lounger, whose French I could understand rather better than that of most of the others present. I introduced myself to him and the dark beauty who lay alongside. And then, in tediously predictable fashion, instantly hating myself for resorting to such a wearisome line, I asked him what he did.

I find it a little sad that, as part of normal social interaction in the West, one of the first questions one asks of another when meeting for the first time is: "And what do you do?", generally taken to mean, "How do you earn your living?" – as if the means by which one is forced to work away at something in order to put food on the table really has anything to do with one's special character, aspirations or dreams. In rare cases, of course, there are those fortunate ones who have found the metier by which they can both make a living and fulfil their wildest fantasies, but these are few and far between.

I hope for a day when people are not judged by their jobs, or by what they have, but by who they are. A day in which one can freely ask, instead of "What do you do?", introductory questions such as:

"And you're from where?", "What sort of music do you like?", "Do you enjoy travelling?", "What are you reading at the moment?", and other such personality-revealing queries, leading to conversations on a vastly more superior level to that which is depressingly anchored to reports of long days in the office.

There, at the poolside, in answer to my question, my friendly Frenchman replied that he was a policeman, based at the village of Le Bar-sur-Loup, some eighteen kilometres distant, from which a weekly patrol car made its round of the local villages.

'So it's your day off, then?' I casually enquired, as he sucked long and hard on his cold beer.

'Not at all!' he replied, 'but I never get much further than Geronimo's pool during the summer months, it has to be said.'

Amused, I was once again struck by the differences between the British and Mediterranean approaches to life. One might say he was slacking, but given the tightly-knit communities of the region – in which everyone looks out for everyone else, and in which the last-known crime had been the theft of a number of flower bulbs from a roadside during the night – one can hardly blame the chap for applying a bit of commonsense to the situation in which he found himself.

Chapter 15

By the beginning of August, back on site, we already had the first floor constructed across the tops of the basement walls, thereby providing a platform from which to build the upper two levels of the house.

It was immensely educational for me, used to English brick-building methods, to participate in the construction of a house in the local Provençal style. The basement walls along the two juxtaposed sides of the house which were effectively cut into the mountain served as a ninety-degree retaining structure. They had been constructed with hollow thirty-centimetre-wide concrete blocks, along with all internal walls joining them at right angles, as buttress reinforcements. The hollow blocks were built up like Lego, within which were laid both horizontal and vertical steel rods at every juncture. The usual practice is to lay perhaps five or six courses of these blocks to form a wall of a little over a metre in height, after which concrete of a fluid consistency is poured into the hollow structure. Having allowed it to set, a further section is then built up, and so on; apertures for doors and windows being formed in the process.

Well, in a gallant attempt to save time, and therefore costs, Gary had decided that we would construct the entire height of the basement walls, thirteen courses in all, before filling the blocks with concrete. This was hugely risky, as the downward pressure created by the weight of two and a half metres of vertical liquid concrete would put unknown stresses on any weak points in the wall, especially at the base. Gary appeared to be confident in his technique, however, and was largely proved to be correct.

The ready-mixed concrete was ordered, all five lorries' worth, each lorry arriving with a powerful pump and forty metres of fifteen-centimetre diameter flexible pipe, through which the concrete would be pumped into the gaping mouth of the hollow wall. We erected scaffolding around the entire perimeter of the structure and I crossed my fingers as Gary and Barry together hoisted the end of the heavy pipe into position over the first part of the wall to be filled, the long grey tube looking for all the world like the snaking trunk of a gigantic mechanical elephant.

The lorry driver switched on his pump and the pipe instantly came to life, convulsively lurching about as the viscous liquid began to surge along its length. It was all two men could do to prevent the thing from wrenching itself out of their hands as the first of the sticky, wet slurry exploded into the cavernous void. As the level of the concrete rapidly rose, the builders had to somehow manage to move in a steady progression along the scaffolding, filling up section after section of the deep, vacuous structure.

For a few minutes all went well, then, suddenly, as the couple stood wrestling with the mighty weight and power of the spewing concrete ejaculation, a loud "bang" resounded from the base of the wall. The ghastly sight of a rapidly-swelling pool of liquid concrete met our eyes, expanding with startling swiftness as it streamed from the hole it had blown in one of the blocks at ground level. Paul and I, having been primed for just such an eventuality, ran around like lunatics, shovelling the spill manically into wheelbarrows to be used elsewhere, whilst simultaneously attempting to plug the breach with used cement bags, rags, or whatever else occurred to us or that we could lay our hands on.

And so the process continued: the two men desperately battling to ensure the majority of the grey sludge arrived where it was intended overhead, and us two, below, dashing about in a crazed frenzy as we endeavoured to prevent the whole wildly animated scenario from disintegrating into a fantastic fondue of grey blocks and liquid concrete.

With the basic shell of the lowest level now complete, and the first concrete floor in place above it, we were ready to begin the second floor block-work, which would form the first level of the two-storey house in which the family would make its home. Gary had been right when, speaking to a somewhat depressed me a few weeks earlier, he had said that as soon as the house was "out of the ground", then things would move rapidly, and he hoped to be working on the inside by Christmas.

It was tremendously uplifting to see our house, for which we had worked so hard, actually taking shape before our eyes, on the side of the awesome mountain which we had chosen to be the place for our home. And yet, daily vitiating the joy I felt at the progress we were making was the ever-present worry as to where we were going to find more money when current funds evaporated in a month or two, exacerbated by the continuous stress caused to both myself and Paul by the arrogant attitudes of those we were obliged to work with.

We were addressed as children on a daily basis, and even, on one occasion at least, work we had completed was kicked apart in front of us, accompanied by the words: "That's a fuckin' piece o' shit; do it again". I protested, pointing out that it was my house and I was happy with the way it had been done, but it seemed as if there was no limit to Gary's desperate need to prove his superiority in a pitifully puerile display of swaggering tyranny. Of course, once the job was finished, with life being short and the time we have on this planet precious, I knew that I would never want to waste another moment of my life in the company of such social inadequacy. But, for the moment I worked on, endeavouring to ignore the man's personality problems, while benefiting from his considerable building expertise, which was, after all, what we had hired him for.

The unceasing stress caused by the situation was starting to make itself felt, however, not only as a tightening coil of dismay within me, but also by spilling out into the evenings, as I attempted, in vain, to prevent my anguish from warping my responses to the trivial differences inherent in family relationships. I drank to counter the daily despondency, often two or more bottles of wine in an evening, and my long-suffering wife, being the one who shared my living space, became the one who witnessed the dangerous depths to which I was sinking.

One Friday, after a day that witnessed a particularly wearing combination of hard labour and depressing atmosphere on the building site, I returned home late, having spent an hour in the bar opposite our apartment, in which I had been treated to several drinks by the ever-hospitable villagers. Karen was rightly miffed on my tardy return, as usually, with three children now in the house, I would assist with the baths of Emily and Tom during the evening, or, alternatively, cook the dinner, while she occupied herself with the children's needs. That evening, with my temper not only frayed but totally unravelled, and hers likewise, due to my unusually inebriated state on arrival, sparks flew phenomenal.

Thus it was that, at eleven o'clock or thereabouts, I stuck my nose in the air, declaring my infallible invincibility in the face of all that would crush me, and stormed theatrically out of the flat. With a duvet in one hand and an abruptly refilled glass of wine in the other, I swayed alarmingly as I made my way off towards the only place in the world that I now felt was truly my home.

I was awakened by the searing heat of the sun blazing full in my face from a sheet-metal sky, and simultaneously sensed the rasping agony of a throat as dry as the Sahara. I found myself flat on my back, arms splayed in mock crucifixion, lying prone upon a bed of simmering steel rods, which, in turn, were arranged across a floor of fiery concrete. Dante would have loved it.

After confrontations of the evening, it seems, the light of morning pours calming rays of commonsense upon all agitation and, as the village church bell struck ten o'clock, I retraced my steps along the route I had so wildly made my way along some hours before. And now, with head hung low and dragging a soiled duvet in my wake, the stormy defiance of the night evanesced into the pathetic likeness of a pitiable character from the strip cartoon Peanuts, and I gingerly ascended the stairs to make peace with my wife.

Chapter 16

August the fifteenth is a major event during the Catholic year, and gives rise to yet another excuse for partying across the Latin world. It is the day, apparently, on which Mary, the mother of Jesus, having been dead and buried for some considerable time, sat up and decided that she had had enough of her dank and dreary surroundings, and thought it might be a good idea to spend some time on the outside. However, a cursory study of Catholic tradition will throw up any number of potential dates and possible explanations of its origin, depending in which particular written document one chooses to put faith, there being, in my experience, numerous variations and suggestions as to which is correct.

In Gréolières, as is the case with other villages littered across the vast expanse of the country, the religious overtones appear to have been forgotten, to be replaced by a three-day music fest. A huge marquee is erected in the village centre, playing host to a miscellany of live bands, to which the people flock from miles around for dancing and alcohol on the cheap, eagerly eyeing up all those who may be from, in the words of Geronimo, "the next village".

It has about as little to do with Christianity as does Christmas, the desires of the flesh playing an obviously prominent role as all and sundry let their hair down for three crazy nights of the year. Young and old alike gather to drink and party, celebrating life and friendship in an intense demonstration of community, while alcohol, weed or nicotine enhance the senses of those looking for a good time, village-style. Ingeniously, the neighbouring villages have developed an integrated approach to the festival timetable, presumably wanting to maximise income from the revellers in the vicinity, and it is usually the case that the event is reproduced in a programme of succession. Thus one is able to spend three nights celebrating in one location, followed by three nights in another, and so on, depending on how far one is prepared to risk one's driving licence, since the journey home becomes progressively extended; unless, of course, one has managed to find accommodation in the bedroom of that person from "the next village".

Many communes in this society-based country have a committee, funded partially by the public purse, whose express function is to arrange parties. I could not think of a better way to spend our taxes, and I ensured that we made full use of the facilities provided. In fact, on a remarkable number of occasions throughout the year, one is treated to an aperitif in a public place, the nominal reason for which is the anniversary of the death of some saintly chap or other, but which in actual fact becomes just one more reason to party.

One such celebration takes place towards the end of the summer, during which water plays an integral part in the festivities. As we took a stroll through the village one quiet Sunday afternoon, we rounded a bend in the road to see, strung across the road and impenetrable, a throng of what must have been at least half the villagers in a rather advanced state of intoxication, and soaked to the skin. Long tables had been arranged along the length of the *lavoir*, the medieval washing place, through which mountain waters still flowed; various vessels stood around ominously. As the family approached, we were treated to a sprinkling of water and the customary "*Bonjour*", leaving us perplexed as we accepted the proffered whisky.

It transpired that this was some ancient festival which utilised the throwing of water to keep away the presence of evil spirits, causing me to marvel at the lack of commonsense that allows mortal beings to cringe in fear of that which is frightened thither by a few watery droplets. Honestly, if anything existed at all that was both invisible and omnipotent, I hardly think it would be spending its time frolicking around the public washing place of a small mountain village. One can think of far more naughty things to be doing given a cloak of invisibility and the benefit of limitless magic powers.

Being in a rather naughty mood myself at that moment, my gaze was transfixed by the sight of numerous young women garbed in what had now become very wet t-shirts. Karen chuckled at yet another demonstration of the enormous sexual power with which women control the world, and slapped me affectionately on the thigh.

Chapter 16

The "Ball" on the fifteenth of August kicked off at about ten o'clock in the evening and was expected to last until at least four in the morning, we were told. As we had already previously discovered, the most striking feature of the whole affair for us was that no generation gaps existed, and we duly rolled up with all children and babies in tow. Old-timers danced with teenagers, children with adults, and the live rock band played cover versions of everything from Jimi Hendrix to Charles Aznavour.

And then suddenly, halfway through the evening, the floor was dramatically cleared for the appearance of the campest scenario I had seen since Julian Clary decided to name his live British tour *My Glittering Passage.* Pouting affectedly, one hand on hip, a handsome, slim, dark man of about thirty years of age, with shaved head, minced into the centre of the dance floor and grabbed a dining chair by its back in passing, which he placed in the centre of the arena with the graceful swirl of an accomplished gay matador. The band, having been momentarily silenced by this wildly theatrical entrance, suddenly struck up a sleazy stripper theme, and our flamboyant friend launched into a hilariously overacted dance sequence, manipulating the chair as a partner or prop, occasionally straddling it in the most humorously suggestive contortions one could imagine.

It was pure Bowie and Ronson from the days of Ziggy Stardust, and yet it was received with liberal good humour and applause by all present, young and old alike.

We introduced ourselves to him and his partner later that evening and gained two more very colourful friends in this camply cosmopolitan couple, Christian and Laurent, further deepening my conviction that we had chosen a unique and special place in which to live.

September arrived, and with it, the beginning of the school year for Francesca and Emily. Although Emily was to settle in relatively quickly, it was quite a different matter for Francesca. Having finally arranged a place for her at the Collège St Hilaire in Grasse, assisted by the ever-helpful Claudine from the *auberge,* the foreign timetable was understandably difficult for her to adapt to.

Most secondary school lessons in France start at eight o'clock in the morning and last until five o'clock in the afternoon. On the other hand, there is no school after midday on Wednesdays, and the summer holidays are a generous two months long. However, Francesca's school was seventeen miles away and the roads in between narrow and tortuous. It transpired that she would have to be at the bus stop at twenty to seven in the morning, rising at the ungodly hour of six o'clock. This inevitably led to us insisting on early nights during the week, which was to prove difficult to enforce in the case of a strong-willed twelve year-old.

I started to assure her that when I had been her age, I rose at 5.30am to deliver newspapers. However, I bit my lip, remembering that as soon as one reaches that point in life when all lectures begin with the "When I was a lad ..." routine, one is not only ignored, but smiled at in a quizzical way, as if one has begun to lose one's sanity, since of course anything that happened about two hundred and fifty-seven years ago can serve no useful purpose whatsoever to the current generation of the same age.

Poor old Francesca. It was to be a difficult time, and her work suffered as she found it difficult to settle into her new environment, both at home and at school. However, on a positive note, she soaked up the language intuitively – possibly inspired by the importance of communicating with handsome young men in her class – and after six months was speaking French as a native, with no discernible trace of an English accent. It was only a matter of months before I was asking her to clarify certain points of French grammar, the case having earlier been the other way round.

Her early start was matched by a late finish, the school bus not returning to Gréolières until six-thirty in the evening, and obviously by then she had little appetite for homework. We became lenient, given the long days she was attempting to come to terms with and the fact that she was now bilingual at least, and that first year became one of acclimatisation. Technical subjects would just have to be caught up with at the next school during the following year.

Chapter 17

As the colours of the mountains began their subtle seasonal shift into autumnal shades of red and gold, the sound of occasional gunfire was to be heard across the valley as the hunting season got underway.

Unlike England, where "the hunt" involves strange types in ridiculous costumes terrorising small creatures with other, much larger creatures, here in France the forests and trails are permeated on foot by individuals searching for something tasty to put in their cooking pot.

One bright morning, having started on the building site at seven o'clock in order to accomplish as much as possible before the day really heated up, we decided to take a short break and installed ourselves for coffee outside the village bar. Into the square a little later, dressed in heavy green forest wear, walked a man, pushing before him a gruesome burden, splayed in a messy red heap across an old wheelbarrow. The coffee lost its attraction as the hideous form of a partially-decapitated wild boar drew alongside us, its mortified eyes staring directly into mine.

The hunter was a small, slight man, with cropped hair and a broad grin, who introduced himself as Pierre. Indicating his trophy with a wave of his hand, he enquired as to whether we wanted to buy a piece of the animal for our evening meal. Before we could respond, Claudine came rushing out from the bar, waving her hands in the air, telling Pierre in no uncertain terms to leave her customers alone, as she shooed him off the premises.

We smiled as he duly trundled off, only to return through the village at regular intervals for the rest of the day, the creature in the wheelbarrow becoming smaller with each passing visit as Pierre managed to sell off various parts of its anatomy to those he met along the way.

I was later to discover that Pierre made his living from various micro-marketing enterprises and was the purveyor of all sorts of other substances, some the result of a particularly ingenious indoor gardening scheme. In addition, he came from one of the oldest families in the area and appeared to know virtually everything there was to know about the village and its inhabitants. His many-tentacled foray into the world of trade and supply made him a fascinating character to get to know, and once I had become a little more familiar with his twangy regional accent, found in him a close companion of loyal disposition and wicked sense of humour.

During September, I received a call from an old friend in Zürich.

He was an Englishman, who had given up a high-flying job as a partner in one of the world's most prominent accountancy concerns in order to indulge his passion for contemporary art by opening his own gallery in the city centre. He planned to promote the English artisans whom he had grown to love whilst collecting pieces from me during an earlier time.

Martin, along with Graham, another accountant friend of mine, had been one of my most supportive clients during the days when I had had a gallery of my own, and I had always told him that I would be there in return for him, should he need any assistance in setting up his new enterprise in Zürich.

Since he was unable to drive, he was paying huge transportation costs when moving pieces of art from England to Switzerland and vice versa. I suggested that he hire a truck, which I could drive from one country to the other, returning unsold pieces to their creators and bringing new items back to his gallery for the next show. It was the least I could do for someone without whom I might very well not have been in the position to undertake the French project in the first place.

Having already done the drive once or twice before, this time things seemed to be fortuitous. Karen and I had recently decided that, with a dry basement now ready to store things, we could, at a suitable opportunity, return to England to collect the rest of our worldly goods, which were lying quietly in the corporation garage in a Norwich side-street. Martin agreed to the plan and we painstakingly mapped out an appropriate itinerary, which would see a large seven-and-a-half ton truck transport our furniture, along with Martin's new artwork, from Norwich, via the Channel Tunnel, south to Provence. Then, having unloaded our house contents at the building site in Gréolières, it would continue northwards into Switzerland, delivering the artwork to Martin's gallery in Zürich, before returning to Norwich with any unsold pieces from the previous exhibition. We would then say goodbye until the next time, and fly back to our respective homes from Stansted Airport.

There was a slight problem before we started out, in that I could not for the life of me locate the key to the garage that I had rented from the city council all those months before. I rang up Norwich City Council a few days before we left, explaining my predicament.

Attempting a casual tone of voice that suggested I was just down the road – and definitely not calling from the south of France, from where I had been using their garage as a cheap storage facility for the last five months, thereby contravening all the small print on the rent card – I asked them if they had a spare key as I had, er, lost mine somewhere in the city on the way home the previous evening. I was assured that they kept duplicates and, having thanked them, indicated that I would call by in a day or two to collect it. I flew into England on a Friday, collected the largest vehicle I had ever driven, and delicately manoeuvred it through the medieval streets towards the council offices, cautiously driving at a pace slower than that of an overweight, and very elderly, snail. With gout.

By the time I had managed to park the truck, it was nearing four o'clock – finishing time on Fridays – and I was quite breathless when I at last collapsed on to the counter of the property letting department. Having explained who I was, and that I had rung earlier about a lost garage key, I was met with a blank and tired expression from a woman whose head was already at home with a large cup of tea.

'Caaarn't do narfin' aboot thaat, ol' boy; we doon't keep spares, y' knoo.'

'B ... but,' I blabbed, disbelievingly, 'I was told that I'd be able to pick one up! I need to get into my garage!'

'Oi'm shur yew doo, but's too learte noo, anyway. Come back Mondee morn'n an' we'll foind a workman to breek the larck f' yew an' fit a noo one. 'Course yew'll 'aff to pay f'rit y'sulf, y'noo.'

I was speechless. On Monday morning we were scheduled to be heading south through northern France. And, furthermore, I had rung especially to ensure that a key would be available. No, I had to load my things the next day. Through clenched teeth, I muttered a strangled "Thank you", and headed off to the garage in defiant mood the next morning. If they dealt with lost keys by simply breaking off locks and fitting new ones, charging everything to the tenant, rather than simply keeping a copy of each key for which they could make a nominal charge, then I would take matters into my own hands. Such ludicrous inefficiency should be rewarded with cutting independent action, I thought, as I walked up to the door of the old garage with a borrowed shovel, to carry out that which they would have had the nerve to charge me for in lieu of the obvious solution.

The old garage had not been maintained for years; hardly any pressure was required to free the rusty lock from its worm-riddled door. I was rewarded with the sight of our possessions, intact and exactly as they had been stored several months before, suffering only here and there from a slight covering of mildew.

Julie had been a brick in offering to help me and, between the two of us, we loaded the entire contents during the Saturday morning; after which we retired to the nearby Fat Cat for a well-deserved pint of Adnams Southwold Bitter or two.

The long journey south was uneventful, until ten kilometres out of Gréolières when the mudguard of the truck lightly grazed the wing of a tourist's saloon on a tight mountain bend near the village of Gourdon. This lead to further unforeseen expense in the form of six hundred euros' worth of finickety bodywork; exactly the same amount as the excess payable on the truck's insurance. We decided to pay the money directly to the other party, as there was no damage to the lorry and I really did not, by this time, have the energy to pursue another endless chain of paperwork, at the end of which we would be paying the same amount anyway. However, the extra outlay only served to reinforce the dread of bankruptcy, drawing ever closer as our borrowed resources dwindled lower by the day.

On arrival in Gréolières, the actual storage of our belongings involved the use of the crane to lower the unloaded items from the nearest point accessible by the truck down into the structure of the house some eight metres below. It was a peculiar sight to see chairs, tables and other familiar objects being gingerly lowered from the sky, Gary driving the crane particularly skilfully in order to avoid drops. There were wide grins all round when a box tumbled off the levitating palette, scattering videos of an extremely erotic nature across ten linear metres of rough ground.

Chapter 17

With everything finally safely stowed in the lower level of the house, it was time to celebrate the success of the first half of the trip.

Martin, generous to a fault, treated us to a slap-up meal at La Barricade, before spending the night with us ahead of the journey north to Zürich the following morning.

Late one September evening, a few days after I had returned to France having completed the rest of the drive for Martin uneventfully, I received a telephone call from Norwich. It was an artist friend of mine, to whom some months earlier, over a beer in the Fat Cat, I had introduced our friend Ian as the best mechanic I knew.

'Hello, Ben, it's Richard.' His voice was horribly subdued. I felt the imminent threat of bad tidings.

'Ian's had a car accident. He's dead ...'

Ian. Larger Than Life Ian. Big, Cuddly Ian. Rolls-Royce Ian. Vulgar, Loud, Hugely Loveable Ian ... Dead?

Dead?

I was shocked beyond words. What to say? What to do? The sudden and unexpected death of a young, close friend is probably one of life's most indefinable moments. I had nothing with which to deal with this, and silently broke down in a gloomy corner of our ramshackle apartment.

Chapter 18

As the building work progressed on the upper part of the house, I began to be woken at night by searing pains that shot from my fingertips to my elbows. My fingers at these times felt numb and swollen, like bunches of unfeeling bananas at the end of my palms. It was similar to an extreme attack of pins and needles, only, in this case, the feeling would not return for half an hour or more at a time, and I found it difficult to sleep as a result. The autumn mornings found me exhausted, with a deepening cheerlessness brought on by the almost certain knowledge that Gary would launch into vulgar verbal abuse and general negativity the moment we met on site. And, as the mists of late September became a more regular morning occurrence, the murky fog of financial ruin also threatened to wreathe itself about us. Times seemed difficult indeed.

I knew that the pain in my hands, which, as the physical work and use of heavy hand tools continued, gradually developed into a twenty-four-hour affliction, was probably due to nothing more than the common condition known as carpal tunnel syndrome. My sister had suffered from the same symptoms at one time and a simple ten-minute operation had completely resolved the problem: a band of ligaments above the wrist, following the onset of unusual levels of stress or exercise, becomes too restrictive for all the nerves, tendons and vessels that pass through the "canal" formed by it and the bones on the other side. Although having inherited my father's squat, thick-set stature, a random and mischievous gene had seen fit to equip me with pixie's hands and wrists slimmer than a gnat's toothpick.

Earlier, in July, I had paid a visit to my doctor in England during our stay there for the birth of little Tom and, having explained the characteristics of my predicament, he had concurred, diagnosing CTS. However, the waiting time for such an operation was, he informed me, about two and a half years, unless, of course, I paid for private treatment, costing in the region of two thousand pounds. I did not have that sort of money available, and in two and a half years I hoped to be fully integrated into the French health system.

As I was about to leave the surgery, he suddenly recommended that I get a second opinion: he could arrange a quarter of an hour's consultation with a colleague of his at the local BUPA hospital. This seemed strange. I had come to my doctor for the diagnosis of an incredibly apparent condition and had duly received his assessment. Why then the need for another opinion for such a common and easily-recognisable malady? And, if a second opinion truly was required, there were four other doctors sharing the very same building as my own! So why refer me to this friend elsewhere? The answer was not long in coming.

'Oh, and it will cost about eighty-five pounds for his evaluation,' he added, as I recoiled in horror. I had paid thousands into the National Health Service for twenty-four years without letup, and now it all seemed completely worthless. Once again, I quietly felt reassured that our emigration to a country in which hospital waiting lists are unknown, and whose health system is recognised as the world's best, had been the wisest decision we had ever made.

Late in September I finally managed to convince my father to pay us a visit, in order that he could see what we had been doing since leaving England, and also because we had not seen him or his lovely third wife, Phyllis, for several months. He'd had a lifelong fear of flying and, save one short hop during his National Service stint in Palestine in the late forties, had never made an aerial voyage. Phyllis helped him to organise a new passport and I flew over to collect the couple in October, as they exhibited a little apprehension in connection with modern airport procedures.

On their first evening in the village, we took them to meet our friends Lyn and Thierry, at La Pierre à Feu, to sample the delights of Thierry's delicious traditional cuisine. It was halfway through the meal, at around ten o'clock in the evening, when I became alarmed on noticing a raised swelling on the back of little Thomas' head, just above his neck. Having been away for a couple of days in England, it seemed that his small skull had definitely altered in shape since I had last seen him and a lump about the size of half a golf ball now projected from the base of the rear of his cranium. I knew that I could not rest until we had seen a doctor and voiced my concerns to Lyn, who was also the district nurse. She looked at the bump and agreed that it looked a little abnormal, although Tom did not appear to exhibit any form of distress. She advised me to take him to a children's hospital in Nice which was renowned for its efficiency and quality of service.

Thierry attempted to give me directions and we made ready to leave right away, as I had become silently terrified by the ramifications of any such condition of the head in a child of barely three months old. It was at this point that our friends once again demonstrated the unbelievable extent of their consideration towards us. Since we were plainly quite stressed, Thierry told us that it would be better if he drove us to the hospital himself, as he knew the way and he could not bear to think of us becoming lost with the baby in need of urgent attention. It was now getting late but, nevertheless, having told Lyn not to accept any more customers and closing his kitchen, he bundled myself, Karen and Thomas into his four-wheel-drive truck and accelerated off towards the hospital, not less than an hour's drive away. We were deeply touched by his generosity and knew that we had met some very special people in this couple.

At the hospital, Karen and Tom were swiftly taken to see a specialist and were advised to spend the night, following which various tests and x-rays would be conducted in the morning. There was nothing more I could do at this juncture so, leaving them in the capable hands of the doctors, I joined Thierry on the long drive back to the village, where he dropped me off at the apartment at nearly two o'clock in the morning. He refused any offers of payment for fuel, gave me a reassuring hug, and left for home.

The following morning, after a sleepless night, I returned to the hospital with my father and Phyllis in tow and, desperately trying to remain positive, we made our way up to the small room in which Karen and the baby had been accommodated. She was smiling as we entered: a tidal wave of relief engulfed me as I sensed the absence of danger. All the tests, she told us, had proven negative. It transpired that little Thomas had simply experienced an unusually fast growth pattern in one area of his skull, and the doctors reassured us that, given time, the rest of his head would develop into a normal shape around it. And so it proved to be.

We paid the seven hundred euros fee at the hospital cash desk with a credit card and left for home, the importance of the health of our children impressing itself upon us as one of life's primary concerns. Funding would simply have to continue to be found from somewhere in cases such as this. We had now formally detached ourselves from the English system and were seeking provisional help in France, but nothing had been forthcoming at that stage. It seemed the paperwork was endless. And what to do with us? Since I was not actually employed, and therefore not donating via the contributions of an employer, we were technically self-employed. And yet we had no income, or the means for earning it, as the gîte-to-be had not been completed! We seemed to stall between several falls, and had nothing to cover the family's health. It was a further continual cause for concern within our increasingly nebulous framework of existence.

Later in the week, Thierry and Lyn invited the family over to their house for a meal, along with Dad and Phyllis, whom they had taken to their hearts as they had us before. Thierry cooked a series of delicious dishes based around fresh pasta and a selection of autumn game, served with the finest red wines from the region. For the first time in his life, my father tasted venison and wild boar, tantalisingly enriched by the chef's subtly-spiced sauces. It was a touching privilege to share the company of our special new acquaintances with those we loved so dearly, and all present appeared to warm to each other as if old friends, regardless of the barriers of language. That evening will always occupy a significant space in my memory.

Sharing my father's love of wild mountain landscape, there was one place I had to introduce him to before he departed for England. So, on their final day in France, with a buttery October sun gently warming a milky blue morning of soft promise, we set off on the short journey to the Verdon Gorge.

It is difficult to convey the sense of stunned wonder that I experienced when coming across this place for the first time. It is otherwise known as the "Grand Canyon of Europe" and, although much shorter and narrower than its American counterpart, its vertical cliffs, which plunge from the roadside in sickening drops to the river nearly a kilometre below, leave the onlooker breathless at their sight. Such is the extreme nature of the scale and height of these vertical lesions in the landscape, one is rendered speechless as the brain tries to come to terms with the dizzying descents beneath one's feet.

The Verdon River rushes along the floor of this immense cathedral of rocky precipices and towering spires, its sparkling waters reflecting the incandescent blue of the sky overhead. The eye of the beholder is treated to new beauty and rugged grandeur at every twist and turn of the roads that circumnavigate this wild gash in the raw and verdant landscape.

As if cast asunder by a frolicking giant, massive slabs of unimaginably-contorted limestone of continually-changing hue lie heaped and scattered across this unique and spectacular region; the result of mammoth lateral pressures and forces between the moving rock masses during the Tertiary period.

A neat trick on a skateboard is not, in my book, "awesome". The latest video game in a trashy arcade cannot possibly be, truly, "awesome". The Verdon Gorge is unarguably, absolutely and undoubtedly, awesome.

As the day drew to a close and we headed slowly back along the beautiful roads which wind their way from Castellane to Gréolières, we found little left to say as we sat in quiet and humbled contemplation of the grand majesty by which we had been surrounded.

Chapter 19

The long summer finally drew to a close around the middle of October and the atmosphere began to get steadily cooler, heralding the arrival of the instability of November, and the spasmodic rains that always occur before Christmas. As the year nears its end, the weather reverts to a stable, bright, fresh and clear period for the three or four months that also see snow at the ski station, twenty minutes away on the north side of the mountain.

One evening in late November I gloomily trudged into Claudine's bar. I hoped that a couple of beers or so would take the edge off the despondency caused by the ambience on site. Earlier in the day, Joe, a quiet and gentle acquaintance from Cipières, had passed by the *chantier* to see how we were getting on. Gary and I had been on the roof, installing the wooden infrastructure which would eventually support the weight of the reclaimed Provençal tiles we had sourced from a nearby builders' merchant.

'Hallo, Joe,' I said. 'How's it going? Oh, by the way, this is our builder, Gary.'

'Ay, ay,' murmured Gary, in response to Joe's greeting. 'I'm the builder. And the builder is a cunt.'

I had no idea what he meant by this and was somewhat surprised by this self-appraisal. I attempted to make light of things.

'No, you're not,' I contested, hopefully. 'You only think you are ...'

Silence from Gary, and the day had continued in a similarly dispiriting vein.

Claudine soon cheered me up, however, when she asked me if I would agree to be Father Christmas for the children of the village at a special event that she was planning to hold in the bar during the forthcoming festive season. I was touched to have been thus chosen – unless it was my gnome-like stature and burgeoning portliness that had influenced her decision, of course – and thanked her for the privilege. I mentioned, however, that my grip of the language, although improving, would not withstand the onslaught of fifty excited children, and I asked her advice as to what I should say on the day. Even the standard "Ho, ho, ho" seemed like a doomed solution; how on earth did the aitch-less French translate that one?

Nevertheless, a couple of pints and half an hour's lesson on set phrases from Claudine later, I emerged from the bar in raised spirits, eagerly looking forward to my new role. I sadly wished that some of the English people we had met in this marvellous part of the world could be half as humanly openhearted as the French friends we had grown to know and love.

Karen, having a particular attraction to all things theatrical, lost no time in locating a suitable costume for the occasion at a knock-down price; a gift with which she was particularly blessed. We proceeded to make preparations for the special day, being careful not to let Emily, then three and a half years old, know of my future transformation into St Nick himself.

Early in December, I spent whatever time I could find – in between building and helping Karen with the new baby and the other children – in my continued battle, with dictionary in hand, to unravel technical letters from various institutions in the hope of finding some sort of state health cover for us all. We also finally managed to compile a dossier to present to various English and French banks in order that we might be able to secure a further loan to continue with our immense project.

But our efforts were to be in vain, as English banks were nervous of a foreign property as security – and an unfinished one at that – and French banks would only loan against a regular salary, quite sensibly, but which of course we did not have. The dark mornings of early December seemed blacker than normal, and it was all I could manage to drag my hungover head up the road at seven o'clock in the morning to do battle with the monsters on the building site. At least, however, the shell of the house was virtually complete and we would soon be working on the inside.

It was as an act of final desperation that Karen turned, once again, to her father for help. Throughout our lives, we had both been independent people, and I found it incredibly embarrassing that she was now having to ask her parents for financial assistance.

Chapter 19

I recalled the first day that I had ever worked for an income. I was thirteen years old and had secured a local paper round, entailing a four-mile round trip at six o'clock in the morning, in the suburbs of Norwich. The area was known as "Hellesdon", and it certainly took on all the horrors of an eternal torture when one was seated on a forty-year-old dinosaur of a delivery bike, rendered completely unstable by the enormous weight of fifty newspapers stuffed into the anachronistic basket slung over the small front wheel. It was a bulbous black behemoth of a machine, with just one, unoiled, extremely high-ratio gear-wheel: I would return home at eight o'clock, dead on my feet, staggering through the back door of our small house to find my mother making packed lunches for the three of us preparing for school. I'm sure I could have held my corner in any Monty Python personal-recollections-of-morning-suffering discussion...

At the end of the first week, I returned home clutching the hard-won trophy of fifty pence to my breast, only to be met at the door by my mother who, always finding it hard to make ends meet, promptly asked if she could borrow it for a loaf of bread. I forced myself to recall how she had sold her own engagement ring just two years earlier in order to afford the new uniform for my grammar school in Thetford, and I quietly relinquished the money.

However, from that moment on, I knew I was on my own from a financial point of view, and the seeds of independence were planted within my soul.

Back in the village, things were getting desperate. We had a hundred and thirty-five euros left in the world, and even that had been borrowed. I finalised my dossier, complete with an exact report on our research, the problems we had unexpectedly encountered to date and photographs of the half-finished house. I also incorporated a market valuation from a local estate agency, which confirmed the projected value of the finished property along with its enormous letting potential. With a recommendation from Karen's father, who also generously agreed to underwrite any forthcoming loan with the offer of one of his own properties as security, the whole package was presented to the Allied Irish Bank in Dublin. Following a few weeks of further tortuous questioning, they finally agreed to advance a commercial loan of a hundred thousand euros, the figure estimated by Gary to be sufficient to complete the house and get the business rolling.

This promise of final funding was the best Christmas present we could have possibly hoped for, and the festive season kicked off in Gréolières with us in buoyant mood. And thus it was that I was in higher spirits than most on the morning of my metamorphosis into Father Christmas himself.

I arrived at the *auberge* with half an hour to spare, and Claudine led me upstairs to an old hotel room above the bar in which I could assume my disguise. Twenty minutes later, I descended, unrecognisably, or so I hoped, with a fat cushion enhancing the rotundity of my natural corpulence and a huge, whiskery, white beard concealing the lower half of my face. With my red velvet hat pulled down low over my brow, it definitely seemed, as I contentedly assessed the overall result in the ancient mirror behind the bar, that the disguise would fool even the closest friends we had made in the village.

I installed myself upon a little stool facing the bar and a bemused Claudine. Beside me, a wooden table groaned under the weight of a gargantuan pile of sickly-looking sweets in plastic bags, their lurid contents apparently reward for those children who could convince me that they had been well-behaved during the course of the previous year. As the first to arrive entered this bizarre arena, parents attempted, for the sake of their children, not to collapse about the place in manic laughter at the crazy Christmas caricature perched uncomfortably before them. Conversely, the faces of their offspring gawped disbelievingly at me in genuine awe, as their tiny brains struggled to come to terms with the fact that He had actually come to Gréolières!

The first child, a little girl of not more than three years old, cautiously approached me at her parents bidding and I attempted to reassure her with a jolly: "'O, 'O, 'O," in the best combination of gruff voice and French accent that I could muster. Screaming, arms flailing wildly, she turned tail and fled, terrified, the length of the barroom and into the arms of her waiting mother. I was going to have to improve my technique ... and fast. The second, a small boy of around five years of age, appeared similarly wary at first, but the attraction of a bag of vividly-coloured goodies finally overcame his trepidation, and he let me haul him on to my lap as I hastily altered the position of the cushion under my scarlet tunic in order to accommodate him.

'T'étais sage?' I enquired, as the beard started to detach itself from my face, my mouth suddenly finding itself swamped with nylon tresses of artificial white moustache. A ripple of giggles flowed through the room and, as I made the necessary adjustments, a queue of now smiling children began to form in front of me, eagerly awaiting their sweet surprise and laughing at this strange, but now apparently harmless, creature seated before them.

After half an hour or so, just as I was really getting into the swing of things, and rather enjoying the feeling of benevolent omnipotence that all deities must experience from day to day, Karen strolled into the bar with Emily in tow. Emily had been informed that very morning that Père Noël was coming to see her in the afternoon; the child fortunately making no connection between my sudden absence and his miraculous appearance. However, as her mother led her towards me, Emily was overcome by a fit of the nerves and absolutely refused to approach the bizarre personage posed awkwardly on the stool in front of her. There I was, having handed out sweets to forty or more children of the village, and my very own daughter was the only one who stubbornly refused to sit on my lap, regardless of any cajoling conjured by the Father Christmas section of my brain. She inched forwards, her nervous gaze fixed intently on mine, and stared hard at what little she could see of my face. Her own contorted in horror at some sudden vague recognition of something familiar within that bearded visage, and she ran from the barroom in terror. There will always be, I suppose, a limit to the extent our children can be expected to buy into fantasy, and Emily had definitely reached hers.

By this time, the parents present were in a jovial mood, having partaken of their own Christmas spirit around the bar and, when I politely requested a beer, several collapsed in bemused merriment at the very idea of Father Christmas needing a stiff drink to sustain him in his labours. Smiling, Claudine's husband Manu passed a beer towards me along the lines of giggling onlookers, but it was only when I held it in my hand that I realised it was going to be impossible to drink through the impenetrable whiskers and hanks of beard that curtained my mouth. There was no way at this point that I was going to destroy the flimsy faith that the children had placed in my presence, and therefore removal of the disguise was not an option. Watching my struggles with the glass, and already perceiving that which passed through my mind in the protection of youthful belief, all present fell apart in hysterical yuletide mirth when I politely requested a straw as the answer to my dilemma. I silently sipped at my beer through the articulated plastic tube, which I passed between the hairy white whiskers of my disguise, and the children gazed on perplexedly, unsure of this new move on the part of Father Christmas. They became totally baffled when I thirstily asked for a refill.

However, it appeared to be generally accepted in good humour by the adults gathered, and the day drew to a satisfying close as I slipped away to resume my own persona in the cramped confines of the little chamber over the bar.

It was towards the end of December that powerful forces within me, having lain dormant for several months following the birth of little Thomas, being suppressed or overcome by stress and fatigue, suddenly re-surfaced. The hot blood of desire was perhaps restored by the jollity of Christmas and the relief drawn from the knowledge that we were able to continue with the construction of our new home. Karen, too, having experienced an extremely traumatic time bringing Tom into the world, followed immediately by the sanity-sapping efforts of acclimatisation into a new and strange environment, was now showing signs of physical renewal and subsequent carnal desire.

One snowy, Christmas-card morning early in the new year, with Francesca and Emily at school and the new baby sleeping peacefully, we found ourselves with a precious few moments together, sipping tea quietly as the falling flakes outside complemented the cosy ambience radiated by a crackling fire in the hearth. I searched – with the experience gained from two marriages, numerous other relationships and nearly two decades of fatherhood – for the magic words which would render me irresistible. Failing miserably.

'Are you thinking what I'm thinking?' I absurdly blurted, my huge hopes of ravishing romance collapsing in a sad cliché as I desperately searched for a positive response in my wife's eyes.

Her answer was silently emphatic. Releasing her bra and removing her underwear with the sort of swift movements that teenage boys think they've mastered by the age of seventeen but which, in actual fact, every man fails to properly accomplish after forty-five years of practice, she pushed me back onto the rug and sat astride me. I needed about as much encouragement as a rampant rabbit presented with a partner made of carrots. We coupled frantically, urgently, hotly, on the floor, across the bed, on the stairs. Again and again, at every available juncture throughout that marvellous, life-affirming day. Thomas thankfully remained asleep during what became a noisy and explosively celebratory expression of our love for each other. Or, more realistically, a noisy and explosively celebratory release of several months of simmering sexual tension.

Karen was breastfeeding Tom full-time, had had no sign of the return of her monthly cycle, and for these and other reasons, we fucked in wild and joyous abandon, safe in the knowledge that we could not possibly be making another baby.

We were making another baby.

Chapter 20

As the winter weather settled into crystal-blue days and sharp, indigo, star-studded nights, we began the interior work on the house which would transform the shell that we had constructed into habitable accommodation. Gary had been right: we were "inside by the New Year", and it felt hugely satisfying now to be working on the preliminary stages of the plumbing and electrical circuits. The massive hammer drills we were using to cut seemingly endless channels for cables through the concrete walls and floors meant tired arms all round, but things were now moving on quickly and I was elated to see the house's circulatory systems slowly threading their way throughout the body of the structure.

One calm morning, as I contentedly chased a groove through a wall to take an electrical conduit, my thoughts returned once again to my father and how much I owed him when it came to not only academic tuition, but also a whole lifetime of practical skills: the things he had taught me since childhood and which were now proving to be so valuable.

During my childhood, my family was never comfortably off. My father preferred to read Shakespeare (his ability to accurately quote whole acts after the requisite number of ales was widely acknowledged) and to listen to the marvellous music of Beethoven with a glass of port in hand, rather than spend superfluous hours in the office pursuing financial rewards.

Nonetheless, he was a master draughtsman (his lifelong métier), gifted with the most exquisitely handsome handwriting that I and many others had seen, could compose enchanting poetry after the tradition of Rupert Brooke, Keats, or Wordsworth, was a good sailor, golfer and mechanic, and had a rich and mellow singing voice, although, admittedly, his repertoire was limited to Italian opera and Bing Crosby. He had even scored a goal during a trial match for Watford Football Club in the fifties, so diverse were his skills. He taught me how to plaster walls when I bought my first house at the age of twenty-one, gave me tips on re-wiring, and installed a complete central-heating system in the family home virtually single-handed.

The unusual thing about Dad was that he was actually very good at, not one or two, but all of the above, and incredibly modest with it, so that, due to his lack of worldly ambition, very few people really understood how exceptional he was.

Thanks to his input, however, and the sense of urgency that I had inherited from my mother ("Never put off till tomorrow what you can do today"), I was now achieving something special, and it was with joyful eagerness that I looked forward to my father's second visit to our new home. January the 23rd was going to be the big one – my fortieth birthday – and it had been arranged that my younger brother, Gideon, would also fly out for the celebrations.

We spoke to Claudine, who asked me which were our favourite beers so she could provide appropriately for the Englishmen who were due to arrive. In her inimitable generosity she wanted to ensure that we had a good time, and offered the use of the bar, free of charge, for a party to mark the occasion. We invited those in the village who had become our friends and I was beginning to anticipate the event with relish. In spite of all the hardships we had endured up until that moment, I was finally feeling a measure of fulfilment, having made a secret vow to myself a few years earlier to the effect that I would endeavour to begin a new life in Provence before my fortieth birthday.

I had not seen Gideon for several years, as he had been spending some time travelling around the globe, and as I started work on the morning of the 22nd of January, I was feeling rather emotional ahead of the trip to the airport to collect the two of them later in the day.

At around eleven o'clock, just an hour or so before I was to leave for the airport at Nice, Barry's mobile rang, shaking me from the reverie in which I had become submerged. He shouted to me above the sound of the power tool I was using, saying that it was Karen: she needed to talk to me. Financial limitations had led to my dependence on other people's mobiles at that point and I was thankful for their long-suffering in that regard.

'Ben? Firstly, don't worry, but Gideon has just called me from Liverpool Street. It seems your dad's a bit late and he just wanted to know how close to flight-time they could safely arrive at Stansted?'

Chapter 20

My father lived in Hatfield and had taken the train to King's Cross early in the morning. Gideon lived in Bethnal Green. He had asked Dad if he should meet him at King's Cross, so that he could accompany him to Liverpool Street, from where they would board the Stansted Express together.

'Don't be ridiculous!' my father had admonished his younger son. 'I was using the tube for twenty-five years before you were even born! I'm sure I can manage to get from King's Cross to Liverpool Street; it's no distance at all!'

And so Gideon had been awaiting his arrival at the Liverpool Street underground exit when he had called Karen.

A bit late? It seemed bizarre. My father had spent many years living and working in London; his knowledge of the capital was profound. He had been looking forward to the holiday with relentless enthusiasm and his wife, Phyllis, was an expert in organising the affairs of her somewhat traditional husband. She had seen him off before taking a long-distance coach to visit friends in Devon. I handed Barry's phone back to him and resumed the work from before.

When, after another forty minutes, it rang again, a small shudder of dread shivered through my being, and my breathing became strangely accentuated. An automatic psychological survival mechanism was kicking into place.

'Hi, love ... he's still not arrived at Liverpool Street. They've missed their flight. Gideon's going to wait until your dad gets there and then he'll call us before catching the next flight. Don't worry; it'll be alright. He's just missed a connection or something. I'll get back to you as soon as I know they're on their way.'

'There's something wrong,' I said to the other builders, as another half hour ticked by. 'It seems my dad's got lost ... or something.'

'Oh, my dad is always forgetting things these days,' said Gary, in an effort to reassure me, but his words fell uselessly to the floor.

My father was fit and healthy. I knew that if Paul (God I was missing his company!), whose mother had recently been killed in a freak hit-and-run incident in Cyprus, had not resigned from the building site at Christmas due to unbearable attitudes from others, he would have known and understood exactly what terrifying thoughts were now shooting, comet-like, across the stupefied universe within my head.

It was at that moment, in the company of two of the most disagreeable people I had ever had the misfortune to meet, that a wordless certainty, a formless horror, grew and pervaded my consciousness. My father's face before mine, I dropped the tools and, as if walking in a coma, drifted towards the windows overlooking the valley. At that exact instant, the low clouds were moved by a sudden breeze, and large raindrops began to fall before my watering eyes.

As Karen staggered, sobbing, screaming, down the steep, muddy slope towards the door, clutching baby Thomas desperately to her breast, my anaesthetised senses were somehow already aware of the ghastly news she bore. Her weeping face struggled to form the dreadful words.

'Ben! You've got to come with me ... your dad's had an accident ... he's ... he's ... dead ... Oh my God ... '

I stared numbly towards the rain-washed sky and pulled her trembling head on to my shoulder. I felt nothing. There was nothing. Deep, extreme emptiness. The world and all around receded into a grey vacuum.

All was still. All was lost.

As zombies, we ascended the slope to the car, while from behind me, Gary kindly assured me that he would look after everything in my absence, or words to that effect. I wasn't hearing.

We entered our apartment, and Karen's amazing level-headedness in times of stress manifested itself in the form of endless calls to the airline company in a frenzied effort to get me back to my brother that afternoon. It was only then that the enormity of the situation finally descended upon me, shattering the fragile protection created by extreme shock, and I crumpled in distress, anger and screaming confusion. Such harrowing moments are shared by us all at some point in our lives, but the nauseous paralysis caused by the actual reality is impossible to convey.

Complicating this particular situation was the fact that no-one knew how, why, or where he had exactly died; only that, after exhaustive enquiries by my brother, his body had been found at the bottom of a stairway in King's Cross Underground during the rush hour. He had been alone. Absolutely, finally alone.

Chapter 20

We knew no more. And now I had to make the journey to the airport, not as previously envisaged in an expectant state of love and welcome for my dear old Dad, but in order to return to London myself, through dark, rain-streaked skies, to a hospital mortuary, to identify his body.

Chapter 21

Ten terrible days in London and Hatfield, with mind and body sustained or distracted by alcohol and narcotics, were enough to partially solve the mystery of my father's death and complete the accompanying administration.

It seemed that, due to refurbishment works at King's Cross, the ticket office had been moved to a temporary position in the station, the new location of which was indicated by a rather confusing system of paper signs and arrows on the walls. It appeared that Dad had been attempting to find the office when he had met his death.

Gideon and I wanted, or rather needed, to see where he had died, alone in a vast crowd of seething humanity, so that maybe we could understand a little of what had happened on that dreadful day. His body had been found at the bottom of a concrete stairway: had he been jostled in the crush, the morning commuters giving no thought to an elderly man carrying a large travelling bag, and then tumbled back down the hard steps? This was almost too awful to contemplate.

The lack of information was depressing but there was, at least for my brother and I, a burning desire to find some sort of answer. We both needed to lay to rest the appalling thoughts and possibilities that kept us awake, night after night, as we lay top-to-tail in the only bed he owned in a cramped studio in Bethnal Green.

Little did we know at that point that an almost unbelievable string of coincidences connecting London and the Riviera would ultimately lead to my mind finding some peace almost exactly a year later, at which time I would finally begin to come to terms with my father's passing.

At least, though, back in London, following a routine post-mortem, we were assured that he had died relatively quickly and painlessly, and that nothing could have possibly been done to help him. This was comforting to know.

During that difficult week or so in town, we were given a couple of tickets for the studio audience of a new comedy show being piloted by the BBC. The Keith Barrett Show proved to be an oasis of light relief in a desert of sadness and, for one evening at least, we were successfully prevented from brooding overmuch on the dark thoughts that persisted in occupying our minds.

Having assisted Phyllis with the funeral arrangements, I flew back to France to collect my family in order that they could accompany me to the small Hertfordshire crematorium to pay our last respects to the man I had so adored. Beethoven's glorious violin concerto, beloved by my father, filled the air as he made his final departure.

Two days later, Karen calmly announced to me that she was pregnant with our third child.

Returning to France once again, the immense sense of loss that I was attempting to deal with threw all our other problems into perspective. But the second death, in just a matter of months, of someone who had been so very close to me only served to increase my awareness of the brevity of existence, and the importance of using what little time we have left in being benevolent to those around us.

One day, soon after I had resumed work on the building site, as I was fitting spotlights into a bathroom ceiling, Barry wandered up, cocked his head to one side and squinted at the two I had just positioned.

'The light on the far side is one centimetre further from the left wall than the next one along,' he ludicrously observed, as if it mattered.

Recent events were beginning to shorten my patience for this endless, puerile criticism, but I attempted to control my emotions, calmly but pointedly remarking:

'Look, Barry, when you've just lost your father, and buried him only a few days previously, you have to understand that whether or not a light is one centimetre off-centre in the ceiling of a rather large bathroom somehow doesn't seem to really be of any great consequence.'

'Yeah, but you can't do anything about your dad being dead, but you can bloody well do something about that light!' he snapped back, walking up to the fitting, ripping it from the ceiling and leaving the wires dangling in sad disarray. 'Do it again!' he concluded, and strode from the room.

His absolute lack of comprehension of the point I was making, coupled with such staggering and unnecessary cruelty, was too much for the weak wall of false normality that I had endeavoured to construct around myself. I descended, shaking, from the ladder, found a quiet corner of the house, and wept. For my dear, gentle father, and the tragedy of damaged lives.

And then, at last, life and levity lifted our spirits in the form of a crazy French-Italian plasterer. Tony had arrived.

Chapter 22

As the interior of the house took shape, we were to meet some wild, but hugely happy and positive, local tradesmen to finish properly the jobs that only a specialist can accomplish. I was beginning to realise that the whole project would have been a lot more enjoyable if I had used French builders from the outset, but at least it was a lesson learned from which I could hopefully advise others in the future.

The first of the professionals to make his mark, both in the standard of his work and in the tremendous improvement he made to the general atmosphere on site, was Tony, a man who I first encountered one evening over a beer or two in Claudine's bar. He was a lean man of medium height, his short, thick, unevenly cropped, mousy hair setting off a gaunt but lively face; the bright, observant eyes and smiling mouth suggested a sharp mind and energetic character. He was accompanied by Cecile, his shepherdess girlfriend, a young woman of fine and comely features whose natural beauty radiated the healthy freshness of her mountainside life.

Having heard of our building project, Cecile asked if and when we would be requiring a plasterer, and when I said that we would be looking for someone during the next week or so, she looked at Tony and smiled. He pulled an assortment of dog-eared photographs from his pocket portraying work he had completed in Paris, and it was of such an unusually creative quality that I asked him if he would be interested in working for us. A toothy grin gave me his answer, and we agreed that he should start the following week.

From the morning Tony arrived at the house, I felt a new and positive energy pervade the place. He brought with him a large ghetto blaster and, placing a CD in its tray, got down to work. I was happily surprised as the opening bars of Beethoven's magnificent ninth symphony exploded at high volume across the room: I saw again my father's face before me. This time, he was smiling, as in days past, dewy eyes closed in rapt concentration as he lost himself in the master's wondrous music. My own tears flowed as I worked alongside Tony, although this time I was filled with joyous, uplifting memories, and I thanked him for bringing the music back into my life.

At the end of the symphony, Tony exchanged Ludwig for a compilation of industrial techno. I grinned contentedly to myself; a man of such diverse tastes was definitely going to add colour to our days from then on.

He was fast, very fast – think Dervish on speed – but the quality and finish of his work was more than acceptable. Of course, Gary and Barry predictably complained at "the crap music, fuckin' too loud 'n all", but we ignored them, sharing a new and buoyant ambience in which to work. However, my enthusiasm at having a fresh, interesting friend to labour with was once again diminished by the depressing attitudes of the other two builders. Every day, Tony would produce exactly the sort of surface I wanted on the walls, but was constantly dogged by Gary, who would make snide remarks over his shoulder as he worked.

'Look, Gary,' I said one day, as I noticed the fires of Tony's excitable temperament being dangerously stoked by Gary's constant criticism, 'he's doing fine. Please leave him alone; I'm more than happy with what he's done so far and it must be difficult to be constantly got at while working.'

'Well, I'm not fuckin' 'appy wiv it,' barked Gary. 'It's my fuckin' reputation 'ere an' I want it done like I want it done.'

'But it's my fucking house! And I'm happy with what he's doing! For God's sake, please just let's get on with it. Look, during the short time we have left, I'll work with Tony and you work elsewhere with Barry, OK?'

A simian grunt signified his agreement to this suggestion, and from then on I endeavoured to ensure that the two were kept as far apart as possible. For the next few weeks, Tony and I occupied ourselves with installing floorboards throughout the upper part of the house, while Gary and Barry started work outside, tiling the terraces and fitting brackets in the walls to take the shutters.

A bizarre overnight trip to England was precipitated by the fact that traditional cut nails for floorboards are not available in this part of France, most interior floors being tiled, or of the more modern, "lost-nail" floorboard construction. Gary had managed to source some flat oak boards of irregular widths at an incredibly good price; they were exactly what we needed to create the comfortably rustic feel we were looking for. However, the heads of screws or headed nails would have completely spoilt the effect, so there was no choice but to take a budget flight back to England for twenty-five kilogrammes of cut steel nails. I would fly into Luton, stay overnight at the cheapest place I could possibly find and return the next day with the precious cargo.

I located a stockist of nails in the town on the internet and, having arrived in Luton, spent the night in a grubby establishment close to a noisy railway line. The following morning, with two hours to go before I needed to head back to the airport, I enjoyed a fried breakfast in a splendidly seedy café close to the builders' merchant as I waited for the doors to open for business. An English breakfast never tastes so good as after a long spell without one, and I felt happily replete as I headed off to buy my nails.

I had the first inkling of complications, however, as I entered the depot and saw little packets of nails and screws hanging on a small rack on the counter. There were no more than fifty nails in each pack ... I needed thousands.

'Mornin'!' chirruped the young chap behind the counter, 'need any 'elp?'

'Yes, actually,' I replied, 'I need about twenty-five kilos of cut nails, about two and a half inches in length.'

The boy took a couple of little packets from the rack on the counter and stared at them, scratching his head.

'I don't fink we've got vat many ...' he cleverly observed, at which point I began to panic. An hour left to complete the mission, and I was stuck with a few ounces of nails and a monkey.

'Look,' I said, 'I've checked your stock on the internet. It confirmed that you've got the nails I need, in the quantity in which I need them, by the box. Twenty-five kilos. And what's more, I've flown here from the French Riviera to buy them!'

'Wha'?! Naaa, yer 'avin' me on, mate. 'Ey, Melv, come 'ere. Got a bloke 'ere says 'e's come all the way from Fraarnce to get some nails!'

Melvin joined us from the gloomy recesses of the world behind the counter.

'Wot? Fer nails?! Fuckin' frogs 'aven't invented nails, yet? Harrr, harrr.'

All-round guffaws. This was not helping.

'Please,' I implored, 'I need twenty-five kilos of cut nails, and I have to be back at the airport in about forty-five minutes. Can you help me?' My desperation must have been blindingly apparent.

'Know wot, Melv, 'e fuckin' means it! 'Ang on, mate, I'll check the stocks,' said the first chap, beginning to operate a keyboard at a painfully inept rate as he stared inanely at the oracle monitor.

I find the blind acceptance with which many computer users believe anything portrayed on a screen in front of them quite disturbing. My man in Luton seems to be taking his time; while he searches his visual display for the answers to all things required, let me take you back to an evening I spent at a new restaurant in Norwich, several years ago.

I had shared a meal with a friend, during which we had consumed three courses and at least two bottles of fine wine. After the meal, it seemed as though we had been overlooked as far as raising a bill was concerned and, being slightly pressed for time, I took my credit card to the all-singing, all-dancing, computerised cash register, greeting the girl guarding it. She took the waitress's notepad and proceeded to enter the items into the machine, then, putting down the pad, looked at the screen, and turned to me.

'One pound eighty-seven p, please,' she said, smiling vacantly.

'What?' I exclaimed.

'One pound eighty-seven p.'

If the owner of the establishment had not been a friend of mine attempting to make it in the catering trade, I would have been sorely tempted to have simply given the brainless girl my card and quietly left, horrified at the dumbing-down effects of modern, mind-saving technology.

'You've just entered all that we had,' I responded, aghast, 'and you're telling me it's only one pound eighty-seven pence? It can't be, can it?'

'Yep, must be. Look. Says here,' said the girl, swinging the screen round to face me and pointing to the figures in the lower right-hand corner, as if I was a complete idiot.

I was later to reflect that it was probably a similarly staggering incident that led to Matt Lucas and David Walliams creating the mindless bank clerk who, given every logical reason to respond in the affirmative, could only respond with: "Computer says no ..."

Little Britain indeed.

Back in Luton, I was reprimanding myself for being just as gullible. I had been foolish to have believed what I had seen on the internet, rather than simply telephoning the company in advance to verify the actual reality. There were not enough cut nails in stock: a series of frenzied phone calls led to a lunatic taxi ride around the town to a series of builders' merchants, my payload of hardware gradually increasing with each stop along the way. I was hot and dishevelled by the time I finally stumbled into the airport and attempted to check in what had now become an extremely heavy, cube-shaped box.

'Any sharp items in the package, sir?' enquired the girl behind the desk.

'Yeah, fifteen thousand nails,' I replied.

'Please be serious, sir, as security is of great concern to all of us.'

'I am being serious!' I blurted. 'Have a look if you want.'

I was escorted forthwith by a nervous-looking assistant to the "Oversize Baggage" scanning machine, in a far corner and hidden from view of the other, normal passengers in the terminal. Having confirmed that the box indeed contained only nails, and was not some sort of sinister, amateur bomb, I was extensively grilled as to my reason for exporting such a bizarre package. It took some time to convince the robots in blue uniforms that I had actually flown to England to buy nails for a floor I was installing in my new French home, and that they were unavailable in that region.

I am sure that, at some time in the future, someone will let me know of a cut nail stockist just down the road from the village, rendering the whole trip completely worthless. It certainly had its entertaining moments, however, and provided a brief respite from the increasingly tense atmosphere of the building site.

Chapter 23

During my absence, Gary had found a quiet English electrician to complete the electrical system for which we had already installed the basic infrastructure; I now turned my attention to finding a plumber to execute the finishing touches to the labyrinth of copper tubing we had laid beneath the floorboards.

One day, as I was drawing some cash from a machine in the nearby town of Pré du Lac, I caught sight of our terrassier, Tony, from Grasse, who had created the original terracing on which the house was now built. We exchanged pleasantries and I mentioned that I was looking for a plumber. He smiled knowingly, and promised to send a good friend of his over to see me as soon as he could.

Two days later, as I was helping the other Tony prepare a huge quantity of plaster for a large wall in the living room, we heard a vehicle descend the gravelly incline from the road to the building site. I excused myself and went to see who the caller could be, to discover a large, unmarked white van parked at the top of the slope which led down to the back door of the house. Suddenly, the doors of the van burst open and, launching themselves from their seats in a cacophony of profanity and mischievous chortling, I was confronted by two enormous men, giggling at some private exchange like two larger-than-life public schoolboys.

One of them was tall, with a large belly that hung, tight in its too-small t-shirt, over the top of his straining jeans. His face was round and boyish; set within it were dark-brown eyes that sparkled with mirth and good humour. He had long, dark hair, pulled back tightly off his face in a neat ponytail; around his feet a small beige-coloured dog yipped and snapped. His colleague, of similar height and build, with broad, strong shoulders, was clad in a yellow t-shirt, over which he wore faded, brown leather dungarees. Across the shirt, in red lettering, were emblazoned the words "Bandidos de France", the import of which I was to fully comprehend in the not-too-distant future. He sported long, brown, grizzled hair, also tied back in a ponytail, while a thick, full beard completed the resemblance of a Carribbean pirate. Only his wide and friendly grin alleviated the apprehension I felt at the presence of this human bear towering before me.

And so Jean-Luc and Philippe, or Big Phil, as we came to name him, became the latest players in the growing theatre of workers at the house. They were plumber and plumber's mate respectively, and provided us with more fun and laughter than we had experienced in months. Each morning they would arrive later than everyone else, in a seemingly continuous state of jollity, nudging and winking at each other as they quipped and frolicked their way through the day's work.

Jean-Luc had quoted for the job of installing the boilers, baths, basins and other plumbing paraphernalia in advance, so it was of little importance what hours they worked, as long as the job got done, and properly. For all their flippancy, the standard of their work was impeccable, and things fell into place smoothly and efficiently.

They greeted us all each day with *la bise*, Big Phil bending to plant a special kiss on Karen's now swelling belly.

This physical contact, sometimes perfunctory, sometimes heartfelt, seemed to me to be one of the reasons for the heightened sense of community in this part of the world. I was now being kissed by twelve or thirteen French men daily, and as a matter of course by many women of the village, which left me feeling, as always, honoured to be accepted as part of their close social circles. There is no generation gap when it comes to *la bise*, and it is rewarding to watch even teenage friends, both male and female, greeting each other in this way. I was also greatly impressed by the manners of the sons and daughters of my adult acquaintances and, whether teenage boys or little girls, each proffered their cheeks for the expected kiss which meant friendship between our respective families.

Sadly, such warmth between friends would be utterly unacceptable in England, on the weird assumption that everyone who has any bodily contact with anyone outside their family circle can only be a rapist or a paedophile. Such absurd, tabloid-fuelled concepts have done nothing to perpetuate friendly relations in the British public at large.

However, I heard a rumour in connection with this custom when performed by adult members of the opposite sex, which occasionally led to a slight sense of either anticipation or apprehension when I was greeted in this manner by the women and young ladies of the village. Normally, one merely brushes the cheeks of one's compatriot with one's own, the kiss floating harmlessly into the ether, unless one is a close friend of the other, in which case one actually plants an affectionate kiss on each side of their face.

But one day, as I was strolling through the village, I passed a very large woman of late middling years, who, in response to my customary '*Bonjour!*', strode over and, grabbing my head firmly between her hands, planted a wet kiss on the corners of my mouth.

As I reeled away from this harmless but novel introduction, I made a mental note to ask someone as to its possible cause. I was in luck, for the next person to cross my path was Pierre, who was returning from a fruitless morning's hunting. As I explained my dilemma, his gaunt face was split by an enormous grin and he actually slapped his thigh as his laughter filled the air around us.

'Ha! You are a lucky man today, Ben! This woman likes you!'

I explained that I hardly knew the woman, although it appeared to be of little relevance.

'When a woman likes you, Ben, *la bise* moves closer to the mouth ... Ha, ha! It is the same for us, too! If it is unacceptable, then simply turn your head further away! If not, you do the same! Either way, they will remember for next time, don't worry! Up to you, my friend! Ha, ha! This lady, I think, though, is not for you, ha, ha, ha!'

And so another little gem of cultural knowledge was filed in the "social niceties" cabinet of my memory.

As the plumbers merrily went about their work, the tension caused by Gary's unreasonable dislike of Tony, the plasterer, was making my life as daily diplomat tedious in the extreme. It reached crisis point at the end of one gloomy afternoon in late February, as I heard a heated exchange taking place between them from the other end of the house; I had been fitting floorboards while Tony was upstairs plastering the walls of one of the bedrooms. Storming down the half-finished stairway, his face flaming red under streaks of drying plaster, his mouth literally frothing from the corners like a rabid dog, he told me, through clenched teeth, that he could no longer cope with the endless stream of verbal abuse being meted out to him by Gary, and left for home.

I found Gary upstairs, running his hand across the wall that Tony had just completed, mumbling to himself.

'Fuckin' crap. Pile o' shit. Calls 'imself a plasterer? Could do far fuckin' better meself.'

'Then why did we bloody well hire a plasterer as you requested?' I asked.

'Oh, er, mmm, well, er, I'm a bit out of practice, tha's all. Anyway, we've got a problem wiv 'is fuckin' attitude. I'll talk to you about it later. I'm out of 'ere.'

He left, Barry trotting poodle-like in his wake, and I remained alone to complete the day's work in peace.

The daily dose of depression served up by the negative attitudes with which I was surrounded was alleviated by my first sighting of a praying mantis, clinging to a wall of the house and fixing me with its alien eyes. Although only about eight centimetres in length, the vivid green of its diaphanous, gauze-like wings caused it to stand out in sharp contrast against the drabness of the wall; I was struck by its strange metaphorical beauty – an exotic emerald illuminating a grey, grey, day.

The day was Friday, and that evening I received a call from Gary.

His tone was subdued.

'Ben? Right, I need to talk to you. Can you meet me at the house tomorrow, say, about two o'clock?'

'Sure,' I responded, 'I'll be there working on the floor anyway.'

The following day, Gary's truck rolled up to the house at the agreed time; he found me nailing down boards in the very bedroom in which his altercation with Tony had taken place. We sat on the warm oak, backs to the wall, facing each other.

'Right, your plasterer's fuckin' crazy.'

'He's a little unorthodox,' I concurred, 'but he's doing a great job as far as I'm concerned.'

''E fuckin' frettened to stick 'is axe in my 'ead the other day; didja know that?'

'Well, he's getting pretty pissed off because he's not being left to simply get on with his job.'

'Yeah, but this is too much. I told my wife what 'e said an' she reckons 'e means it.'

''Course he doesn't mean it! It's the sort of thing you come out with when you're at your bloody wits' end with someone! You don't need me to tell you that! Anyway, your wife hasn't even met him! How could she know?'

'Well, she reckons I should take it seriously. My kids need their farver alive, she says.'

This was such an exaggerated extrapolation of ideas that I began to sense another agenda underlying his reasoning.

'Well,' he continued, 'I've met you today to tell you that I'm not interested in doing the downstairs. I'll work for one more munf an' that's it. Can't work wiv a fuckin' loony around.'

'What do you mean you're "not interested" in doing downstairs?!' I exclaimed.

The "downstairs" was the whole ground-floor level, which was to become the apartments from which we were to earn our living. No work whatsoever had been done therein to that date, and we had hoped to be ready to start letting for the summer.

'But you agreed to build our house for us! You can't just stop halfway through! You estimated completion by the beginning of June, and you're leaving me in the lurch at the end of March, with everything still left to do downstairs? Look, mate, there isn't even any heating fitted in our part of the house, there's no way in which to approach the building from the road, and the lease on our apartment is up at the end of next month. We'll be moving into a cold, unfinished place, and Karen's pregnant, for God's sake!'

''S your fuckin' fault. Anyway, I'm goin' at the end of March. Unless you fire Tony tomorrow.'

There was no way I was going to fire Tony and Gary knew it. Not only had he done nothing wrong, we were also beginning to become firm friends outside the sphere of the building site. The root of the whole problem, of course, was Gary's bully-boy behaviour, his incessant need to belittle others and the quality of their work. In addition to this, I recalled that he had arranged another, higher-paying job for himself when he had completed our house. It was at this point that I began to understand that the whole "Tony" fiasco was probably being manipulated and amplified as an excuse for him to slip out of his agreement with us without appearing culpable.

As I assimilated the possibility of this new, unprincipled aspect of this shady character, feeling somehow cheated by the lack of integrity with which he was sliding out of the contract, I simultaneously began to sense the relief that one feels when emerging from the shadow of a long period of despair. At that very moment, sitting on a half-finished wooden floor, with the winter sun casting its healing rays across the void between us, a small smile of contentment played upon my face as I contemplated the elimination of this particular human being from the landscape of my life.

Later, talking with Karen, as by the hour my spirits lifted at the thought of happier days ahead, she corroborated the fact that I was already appearing more cheerful. However difficult it was going to be to complete the house myself, I felt elated that Gary's underhandedness would at least finally free us from his miserable presence.

Chapter 24

When Tony heard that Gary would be finishing in four weeks, he smiled broadly and thanked me for my support.

'Don't worry, Ben,' he reassured me in his own, theatrical way, 'I'll help you finish this house. We'll do it together and get someone from the village to help us when we need an extra pair of hands. Trust me. The great Anthony will save the day!'

I laughed, and we worked on happily for a few days, until Gary once again surprised me with his relentless arrogance.

'Right, Ben, I'm goin' at the end of March, an' I want my wages now for the last month in advance.'

'What?' I asked incredulously, as bells pealed raucously somewhere in the recesses of my disbelieving brain, 'You're pissing off in four weeks and you want the money for that now?'

'Yep. Er, it's me wife's, mmm, burfday an' I want to take 'er on a foreign 'oliday. Only don't tell anyone about it, 'cos it's, er, well, it's a surprise.'

'I'll think about it,' I said.

Karen chuckled when I told her of Gary's final demand.

'You're kidding! Pay him in advance?' she asked. 'You won't see him for dust if you do.'

'Come on,' I said, 'he may be difficult to like, but he's not a thief. He wants to take Sharon on holiday. It's her birthday.'

'Well, it must be difficult for her living with a man like that. She deserves a holiday. I don't like it, but we can't presume he's going to be dishonest, I suppose.'

So I raised the cash and handed it to Gary during the early part of the month on the newly-finished terrace of the house. As he took the bulging envelope from my hand, I put a question to him.

'So,' I said, 'how about you? Would you pay someone in advance if they were working for you?'

'No, I fuckin' wouldn't,' he said emphatically, and turned back into the house.

Three days later, he was gone. And Sharon got no holiday.

Strangely, or otherwise, Barry disappeared at the same time, with no warning or notice, and subsequently started work on Gary's new job the following week. My suspicions had been correct, and Barry's lamentable need to impress his faux-mentor had sadly overcome any integrity he may have had in connection with his working agreement with us.

As Tony and I battled on to get the upper part of the house completed and therefore habitable before our lease ran out on the apartment in the village, a worryingly low bank balance marred the otherwise vastly improved mood on site and within our family.

The Irish bank had asked Gary for an estimate of the cost of finishing the house back in December, and the hundred thousand euros which they had advanced to us was the direct result of his written calculation of the cost of all materials and labour required to complete the project. So why, with the entire lower level still unstarted, and the upper part of the house barely habitable, unheated and inaccessible from above except by a very steep and muddy incline, was there only thirty thousand euros left to play with?

One of several possible answers was soon to become apparent.

Tony and I sat out on the terrace one fine spring morning to estimate the cost of the remaining work. There were ceilings, walls and floors to install in the apartments, in addition to heating, plumbing and electrical systems, windows, doors, and shutters.

Surrounding the apartments-to-be was a rough, uneven rocky area, which would have to be covered with decking or concrete. Then there were beds, bedding, sofas, chairs and tables to buy, along with televisions, ovens, fridges and other electrical necessities. The exterior of the house was still of grey block and in need of rendering; and there were no stairs up to the front door, which was two metres above the level of the surrounding land. There also needed to be some sort of stairway constructed from the south-facing terrace up to the parking area, twenty-five metres away atop a steep incline. In the upper part of the house, into which the family would be moved in just a few weeks, a fireplace and chimney had to be built, doors and shutters needed to be fitted and kitchen units had to be installed.

Gary had really left us up to our necks in it.

Chapter 24

Tony proved to be priceless. Instead of contracting the exterior rendering work to a specialist concern (Gary had already told me that I could expect to pay thousands of euros for this work alone), he promised me that, with two people to help him, he would do it by hand, within two to three weeks, if we could find some suitable scaffolding. He would also find a means to circumvent the costs of floor tiling, using finishing techniques with white cement and pigments which he had discovered over the course of many years in the building trade. He himself would install the fireplace and chimney with my help, and he would build an exterior stairway from reclaimed railway sleepers. We would do everything ourselves, and what we did not understand or know we could find out from those who did. He re-instilled the confidence in me that had been destroyed by Gary's daily disparagement, and I began to relish the challenge ahead.

However, notwithstanding the costs he promised to salvage for us, he sombrely announced that we would need another fifty thousand euros to finish the house to a standard anywhere near ready for letting. And, although he was willing to work the longest days he could feasibly manage, it was going to take at least another three months to get there.

Following Gary's earlier estimations and promises, the bank was expecting repayments to commence in June. Now, not only were we going to miss the summer season, we were going to have to borrow another fifty thousand euros. The roller coaster of hope and despair was once again sharply descending.

Having experienced the final demonstration of Gary's shifty behaviour, I now allowed full entrance to the nagging, terrible thought that had been knocking on the door of my consciousness since he had deserted us. Although it was us who paid the monthly account at the builders' merchant, it was Gary who had actually done a lot of the ordering, as of course it was he who would know exactly which materials, in what quantities, that we would need for each delivery.

For the first time, I sat down with a pile of yellow invoices and a French-English dictionary and struggled to decipher, not only the technical language, but also the abbreviations of the items on the list.

It was difficult: each month's invoice consisted of two or three pages, with perhaps a hundred or so items thereon, from concrete blocks to wall fixings, from timber to waterproofing paint, cement to insulated plasterboard panels. The lists seemed endless, but with the help of Tony and Big Phil, we eventually began to untangle the unending catalogue of products that had been purchased since May of the preceding year.

The full measure of my astonishing naivety became apparent as we compiled a list of goods which not only had we never ordered, but which we had never seen – paid for by ourselves. Gary had still been in the process of putting the finishing touches to his own house during this time, as well as working on other projects now and again, so where at least some of these surplus supplies had possibly gone was now becoming horribly apparent.

I began to recall seemingly insignificant events on site that retrospectively took on ominous proportions. I remembered, for example, the time that, following the creation by Gary of a beautiful oak beam system for the ceiling of our lounge – an admittedly masterful piece of craftsmanship – a two-metre long, thirty-centimetre square cross-sectional piece of oak timber remained unused. Of course, I wanted to keep this for future use: I had in mind a column for a lighting installation.

'Nice bit 'o timber, that,' remarked Gary, as we congratulated him on how little wastage there was after constructing the ceiling.

'Isn't it?' I agreed, 'I'll try and make something from it when I get some time.'

It was only after about three or four days that I noticed the absence of the beam from the place where I had laid it, alongside one wall of the house, in a relatively sheltered spot.

'Anyone seen that oak beam that was left over from the ceiling?' I asked everyone working that day.

No response. I tried again, and again, until, due to its blindingly obvious absence, someone, I surmised, would have to admit to some knowledge of its whereabouts. I was on the verge of doubting my own sanity, when I approached Gary directly.

'I don't suppose you helped yourself to that piece of oak that I told you I wanted to keep, did you?'

'Yeah, er, well, yeah.'

'But I told you that I wanted it for something later!'

'Tough, innit. What you gotta understand is there's perks, mate. An' that was the oak. Perk o' the job.'

I would have let him have it had he asked me.

A short while later, Gary had ordered the Spanish tiles for our external terracing. He had estimated eighty square metres' worth, and the tiles duly arrived three days later in four large wooden crates.

They were stored at the top of the incline leading down to the house. I had arrived on site the next morning to see that one of the crates had been opened and several layers of tiles were missing from the top of the pile. Not many, perhaps forty or so, but it was enough to cover about five square metres. I had headed down to the house, delighted that Gary had already started on the terrace tiling. He was doing something else. The tiling had not been started.

'That's strange,' I said, 'some of our tiles have gone missing from one of the crates.'

'Wha–? Nah, I don't fink so.'

'Yes, really,' I answered. 'It seems improbable in such a small village, but I distinctly remember that they hadn't been opened yesterday.'

'Yeah? Ah, er, well, you never know, Ben. You can't trust anyone in a French village, can ya? They're fuckin' French. Take anyfing.'

From my experience up to that point, I would have trusted everyone in the village that I had come to adopt as my home. I knew of no one who would steal from us. But even if so, why just a few tiles and not as many as they could get into the back of a hastily reversed van? It seemed strange, but I let it go.

It was only after Gary had abandoned us that I recalled helping him tile the borders of his swimming pool during the first month after our arrival in the village. He had told me that he liked the tiles and would be using them elsewhere on his property. Strangely enough, they had been exactly the same tiles that he had later recommended we use for our own house! He had then ordered the quantity that he felt to be sufficient for our terrace and, even after having some bizarrely disappear immediately following their arrival, we still had exactly the right amount left to cover our terrace ... not too few, as I presumed would have been the case having had some taken from under my nose.

And later, when Paul informed me that he and Barry had been used by Gary to work on his house in my absence, their wages being paid by us, I really did not want to see the loathsome image being formed before my eyes as the pieces of circumstantial evidence began to seamlessly interlock.

I now finally understood why I had perhaps been asked, back at the very outset, to put the builders' merchant's account in my name.

I had been taken for the longest ride of my life. I assimilated all this as best as I could, until one particular small item suddenly emerged from the yellow page of an invoice and, as I re-checked the date at the top of the page, I was forced to turn away, riven by despair.

It was only some firewood, ordered by someone else on our account for their own use. What really hurt, however, was the timing. On this occasion, I had been in London.

Identifying the body of my father.

Chapter 25

We did, of course, make preliminary efforts to establish some sort of proof that might lay the foundations for an attempt to redress the apparent deceit to which we had fallen victim.

We met with the management of the builders' merchant, who finally, after lengthy talks and production of receipts containing those items that we had never seen but paid for, sadly informed us that there was nothing they could do. As far as they were concerned, we had authorised the builder to order goods on our account, and it was not their responsibility if he had possibly been taking advantage of the situation. There was absolutely no proof that everything they had supplied was not intended for our project, and we therefore had little hope of restitution.

Karen's father was kind enough to offer to source a reliable lawyer to take the case further; after all, he had already invested his own money in the development of the affair and, consequently, had lost out along with the rest of us. He also generously proposed, if necessary, to assist us with the funding of any necessary legal action that may be required in order to reclaim that which had been taken from us.

But I was tired. So very, very tired. Exhausted from two years of massive financial losses, weary from a daily bombardment of boorish bullying, drained from sleepless nights due to physical pain and restless infants, weak from long days of intensive labour, and absolutely devastated by the recent, shocking death of my dear father.

I apologetically told Karen, who had become increasingly incensed by Gary's barbaric treatment of others, including his wife, that I simply had nothing left, physically or psychologically, with which to fight my corner. Regardless of what we had lost materially, there was everything now to gain on a human level, and all I wanted was to dump the previous year's anguish on the slagheap of existence, and focus on the days ahead.

I recalled reading – in an outstandingly life-affirming book entitled *Free to be Human,* by David Edwards, PhD – about the desperate struggle for material wealth, which, from birth, this marketplace of a world endeavours to convince us is the only thing worth striving for; such material gains then being contrasted with the priceless knowledge that whatever you have, there will always be something else to want for; thus leading to the endless spiral that is work, purchase, disillusionment, more work, further purchases and continued disillusionment, resulting in an ultimately frustrated demise and a terminal dissatisfaction with life. Meanwhile, those who profit financially from the extreme gullibility of the world's masses become fatter at the expense of all those working for the next product they have been brainwashed into believing will make them happy. Obvious, maybe. Escape routes are less apparent.

I just cannot see the point of spending the short time we are allotted on this "mortal coil" in a frenzied attempt to gather things about us. We leave this life as we entered it; with nothing but the naked body in which our being, our consciousness, is housed. Of what ultimate use, then, are physical manifestations of this thing we call "wealth"? Such squandering of time given, to chase the illusory dream of possession!

In his fascinating study of the parallels between modern physics and eastern mysticism, Fritjof Capra explains the Chinese awareness of the losses caused by the accumulation of things, which are actually of no use along the road to real human contentment:

> "In the Chinese view, it is better to have too little than to have too much ... Just as the man who wants to go further and further East will end up in the West, those who accumulate more and more money in order to increase their wealth will end up being poor.
>
> Modern industrial society which is continuously trying to increase the 'standard of living' and thereby decreases the quality of life for all its members is an eloquent illustration of this ancient Chinese wisdom."

Also recognising that a simple life spells true happiness, the thirteenth-century poet Jelaluddin Rumi wrote:

> "Someone who goes with half a loaf of bread
> to a small place that fits like a nest around him,
> someone who wants no more, who's not himself
> longed for by anyone else,
> He is a letter to everyone. You open it.
> It says, Live."

Friends around one's deathbed at the time of final departure surely have to be so much more valuable than piles of money and the hardened faces of those pillaged along the way.

And so I endeavoured, for the second time in a year, to mentally write off a large sum of money in exchange for peace of mind and the serenity provided by the knowledge that one particularly depressing piece of our environment was no more.

As we drew towards the end of March and the cessation of our lease on the village apartment that had served as the family's home to that point, the upper floors of the house were still unready for our installation, thus confronting us with the unforeseen problem of interim accommodation.

One evening in La Pierre à Feu, while enjoying yet another delicious spread from the gifted hands of Thierry (being aware of our difficulties at the time, he had magnanimously offered to feed us on account), the subject of our temporary housing dilemma came to his and Lyn's attention. Once again, they demonstrated the depth of their friendship as they informed us that they had an old caravan in their garden which, although being somewhat compact, was free for us to use until such time as the house became habitable.

Deeply touched by their beneficence, I pointed out that it could possibly be another month before our place would be at all ready for the family's accommodation, but they simply smiled and told us that we were welcome on an unlimited basis. They even had a small room in their house, which would serve for Francesca, they said, leaving myself, Karen, Emily and baby Tom to share the little caravan. They would offer us the use of their one, small bathroom, and would provide evening meals for us, since there were no facilities in the old caravan itself. We were again moved beyond words at the limitless depths of their genuine goodwill. These were the sort of people in whose company one felt uplifted and invigorated; those who gave of their time, their energies, themselves. It was these people who once again reaffirmed for me the value of investment in human relationships.

As our lease on the apartment in the village expired, we moved the few belongings that we had brought from England in the two cars, aeons previously it seemed, into the basement of the house, to join the plethora of boxes, crates and plastic bags already stored in those concrete chambers below, and shifted the family into the caravan in the garden of our friends.

We left the apartment in an impeccable state, but the landlord was reluctant to refund our deposit, being one month's rent, about seven hundred and fifty euros. He told us that we would receive an itemised list of any retentions, which followed a few days later, causing much mirth at its first airing.

Among the bizarre items listed thereon as missing or damaged, there were:

> 17 pillowslips
> 27 duvet covers
> 15 single sheets
> 25 double sheets
> 38 knives
> and 17 lampshades.

This from a small, three-person apartment! We laughed at such a curiously-concocted confection, and demanded an interview with the landlord. He apologised profusely when he arrived, stating that his agent must have made some sort of error, and promised that a revised version of the final inventory would follow imminently. It did, but in place of the ludicrous items listed above, there were further, equally ridiculous and equally costly articles presented to us, leading to almost exactly the same outcome: virtually none of our deposit would be finding its way back into our already severely depleted bank account. After several subsequent confrontations, we managed to claw back a little more of that which was justly due, but the final result left us, once again, counting costs beyond anything we could have envisaged.

As one chapter in the story of the family's housing came to an end, another one began, and, even if this time it seemed as though we were shoe-horning four people into a Victorian bathing machine, we at last began to feel that things were finally moving towards a favourable conclusion.

The days passed happily. Thierry's son, Baptiste – a tall, wiry and fair nineteen-year-old who bore all the energy, common sense and adaptability of someone with far more experience – joined us on site to complete the team that now comprised Tony and myself, along with the spasmodic appearance of the plumbers and the electrician. Finally, everything felt exactly as it should have done from the start.

Here we were, building our own house, in an unbelievably beautiful setting, surrounded by adorable new friends, within a safe and exhilarating community.

The only hitch now was to find another fifty thousand euros, but that was small fry compared with the problems we had, at last, left behind us.

Chapter 26

Tail clamped firmly between my legs, I re-approached the Allied Irish Bank in Dublin. This time they were, of course, more circumspect.

How on earth, they asked, had we allowed ourselves to get into such a short-sighted situation? I proceeded to catalogue the comedy of errors that had been our fate, and also laid out a further business plan based on a new, professional and higher valuation of the building and its future letting potential. Even so, it must have seemed to them that over the previous few months, as for Mr. Bowie, God had taken my logic for a ride.

However, the photographs and supporting arguments were apparently convincing, as they finally consented to a further advance of fifty thousand euros in order to complete the venture. We were on the verge of realisation, and would only be able to commence repayments to them if the place was functional, and for that and other reasons, I presumed, it was in their financial interest to see the scheme through to its culmination. This new lease of life, coupled with the heady sense of relief I now felt as a result of the hugely improved conviviality on site, lifted our spirits to new heights, and I approached each day's labour with vastly improved levels of energy.

Other things that added to our general sense of all things auspicious included Francesca's sudden improvement in her school achievements, not the least of which was the astonishing news from her teacher that she now spoke French with no discernible trace of an English accent, after just six months at the school. Perhaps the vast congregation of male groupies that trailed in her wake had had something to do with her rapid development of foreign communication skills. The new words dripped effortlessly from the piper's lips, and male rats of both medieval village and city schoolroom swarmed from all corners to stake their claim, spellbound.

The news of the bank's further support naturally needed to be celebrated, so we took the children one evening to La Barricade, for some of Philippe's deliciously palatable pizzas and a bottle or two of good Provençal wine. Being a Saturday evening, the homely restaurant was stuffed to the rafters with village locals, and the atmosphere was, as ever, buzzing with good humour and warm hospitality.

There came a moment when a hush descended upon those present and, as knives and forks were laid down, smiles crept across knowing faces as they turned towards a lean, dark, balding man, whose wicked grin and glittering, black eyes drew the rapt attention of his now eager audience. It was Jacques, or Jacqui, the ironworker, who was later to forge the railings for our terracing, but who was also capable of fabricating an amazing array of fantastic metal sculptures, mad as a box of frogs. The silence in the restaurant now complete, a sense of exquisite expectancy hanging heavily in the air, he began to recount his anecdote.

The reader will, I pray, excuse a slight digression at this juncture in the interest of a little background information, without which Jacqui's story would be rendered meaningless.

The nature of the terrain in these parts, as has been previously described, is a rugged fusion of jagged mountains, wooded valleys and alpine forests. Any film buff will recall the car chase at the beginning of the James Bond film *GoldenEye* in which Pierce Brosnan's ancient but beautiful Aston Martin races (and preposterously keeps pace with), a modern Ferrari driven by a sultry brunette along a spectacularly-situated mountain road, flanked by towering rocky spires and chilling drops to the valley below.

The climax of the scene involves a sharp handbrake turn on a hairpin bend below some ancient ruins, at which point one gets a brief glimpse of a small hilltop village. The village is Gréolières, and the road is the route up to the ski station on the north side of the mountain; the very road on which our house was being constructed.

I had not seen the film until long after we had moved to the area and I was amused, following the car's sharp halt above the village, to see the camera pan upwards from the car to reveal, not Gréolières, but Monaco, panoramically displayed in all its glory!

Later again we were to discover, whilst whiling away a hot summer's afternoon beside a stunningly blue mountain lake an hour's drive to the west, that the dam from which Mr Bond leaps at the very outset of the same film is located between Gréolières and Castellane, and not in a chilly, far-flung corner of a Russian wilderness.

Such scenes perfectly illustrate the sparse reality of flat land in this region; any level areas are jealously guarded and farmed by the families that have inherited them since time immemorial. In fact, it has been said that, to the country people of the Alpes Maritimes, a piece of flat land is of as much, if not more, importance than the wife of its owner.

It is with this particular point in mind that we now return to the hushed, hot interior of the pizzeria, as the storyteller begins his tale:

'There are two old chaps of the valley, chatting about this and that and enjoying the sunshine, when something catches the eye of one of them, and he stares, aghast, over the shoulder of his companion.

'"Oh, my God!" exclaims the old boy, pointing and tapping the other wildly on the shoulder, "There's someone making love to your wife in your field!"

'"Wha–?!" blurts his friend, and, totally shocked, turns abruptly to look for himself. After a second or two, his shoulders lose their tension, he relaxes and, now smiling, turns back to face his colleague.

'"That's alright," he grins, "that's not my field."'

The restaurant dissolved into heaps of laughter at this hilarious comment on their heritage, and I realised that, for the first time, I had fully understood a joke told in French.

Apart from the physical constrictions presented by the confines of the little caravan, we were feeling more positive and relaxed than we had for months, and one weekend decided to have a break, taking the family out for a day at the ski station before the snows disappeared for another year.

Gréolières les Neiges, coming under the same communal jurisdiction as the village itself, is the closest alpine ski station to the Mediterranean Sea, just thirteen miles from the coast as the short-toed eagle flies. This being the case, the snow usually arrives at around the end of the year, but is gone by the beginning of April.

The route from the village threads its way up through startling, rocky holes in the cliff face, which span the road like the abandoned spectacles of some gargantuan stone deity. As the road climbs higher, the views back towards the perched village become increasingly impressive. Care must be taken by sightseers, however, as, for some inexplicable reason, the most impressive vantage points are located on the tightest of bends, where the road is at its narrowest, and overhanging the void below.

It was beneath one such section of the road that we discovered, while enjoying a walk through the forest some months later, the burnt-out remains of a small car, above which, on a series of ledges and outcrops, various pieces of its mechanical anatomy had been deposited, presumably during the course of its horrifying plunge from the road above. Enquiries in the village led to the solving of the mystery, the details of which were provided by the relevant article in *Nice Matin,* the provincial newspaper that Claudine produced for us back at La Vieille Auberge.

Apparently, a wealthy playboy from Monaco had been devastated to discover that his girlfriend had taken another lover, and no amount of pleading on his part would alter her devotion to the new man. In a fit of jealous rage, he announced to the world that if he had truly lost the love of she who made his life worth living, then he would end his now miserable existence, and would be remembered for his final, public martyrdom to the cause of true love. One rain-lashed winter's evening, he drove from the metropolis up into the hills, to the most dramatic setting he could find in which to stage his theatrical departure. Above Gréolières, he accelerated his car towards the gaping emptiness beyond the road's edge and, smashing through the low barriers, man and vehicle plummeted nauseatingly into the abyss, crashing to rest several hundred metres below in a wild explosion of twisted metal and rocky scree.

Walking away with bruises, the unsuccessful martyr stumbled into the village two hours later and shamefacedly asked for a lift back to Monaco!

Beyond the scene of this amusing tale, the road turns sharply to the right, and crosses a col, flanked on both sides by a verdant pine forest through which the rocks, shaped into fantastic forms by the elemental forces of nature, emerge like lofty sentinels of the alpine plateaus beyond.

The first time I took this route, I was absolutely dumbfounded by the clear-cut demarcation between deciduous and alpine vegetation. During winter, there is a bend in the road that marks precisely the lower limits of the presence of snow: it feels incredible to pass between one of nature's finest environmental boundaries and experience such a remarkable change in one's surroundings. Just five minutes from the village on which the sun shines over forested slopes of oak and beech, one enters a bright, green-and-white, Christmas-card world of luminous lakes, blindingly-blue skies and grassy alpine meadows. Silent, sparkling streams tumble through rocky gullies, and the air is heavily laden with the soporific scent of sweet pine and thyme.

A right turn back towards the northern side of the mountain leads to the ski station, nestling in a combe at the base of the imposing Cheiron massif. Just before one arrives at the station, an easily-overlooked ramp to the left of the road leads up to one of the most breathtaking viewpoints in the region. At this point, one leaves the road, having passed through soft seas of pine and fir, to ascend just fifty metres, and be visually paralysed by the enormity of the vista unfolding beneath one's feet. It seems as if the whole world has been spread out before one's very eyes, as the mountainside drops away and down, then plunges skywards in a series of colossal rocky ridges, heaped one on top of the other, receding into the visible distance to every extremity of the horizon. Deep-green valleys, in which nestle toy-town villages, lie beneath skyscraping faces of multicoloured rock, riven by the dreadful depths of dark and mysterious crevasse-like canyons. The Alps ascend before the viewer until they melt into a distant blue haze of sky, snow and glorious illumination.

There are certain places, certain times, which leave one not only speechless, but emotionally helpless. I cannot stand before such majesty without filling up with some sort of heightened sensory awareness, an abandoned capitulation to the immense forces that render the trite tedium of everyday materialistic pursuit pointless beyond words.

As a twelve-year-old schoolboy, I was, perhaps understandably, laughed at when I admitted that, in addition to my obsession with Led Zeppelin, Beethoven, the Sex Pistols and David Bowie in particular, I felt an affinity with the sentiments expressed in the songs of John Denver. Someone, at least, should have helped him with his hairstyle. Thirty years later, however, standing before that immense panorama of boundless space and grandeur, the words from one of his shortest, but most powerful songs were suddenly, and with infinitely heightened new meaning, soaring across the landscape of my awe-inspired mind:

> "Come dance with the west wind and touch on the
> mountain tops
> Sail o'er the canyons and up to the stars
> And reach for the heavens and hope for the future
> and all
> that we can be and not what we are."

All that we *can* be; not what we *are.*

Simple, maybe. Sentimental, definitely. Motivational, hugely.

Chapter 27

April the seventeenth, 2004. The culmination of years of dreaming, planning, change. Having spent six weeks sharing the home and hospitality of our kind friends, we moved, at long last, into the house that we had created, and which would become our dwelling for as long as we cared to think about.

There was still a lot of hard work ahead, but the emotions I felt as I awoke after spending our first night in our new home, to look out of the large windows giving on to an unbroken view of the sun-filled sky pouring itself over the forests and mountainsides all around, are impossible to convey. As a theatre curtain recedes to reveal the colours of the scene behind, any remaining fears of future problems receded from my mind to lay bare the joyous conviction that we were in the right place.

Tony, Baptiste and, from time to time, their young friend Olivier, would arrive at around 8.30 in the morning and greet us with kisses and offerings of food for lunchtime. The ramshackle state of the kitchen in which we shared breakfast was of little importance in comparison to the all-pervading jubilance that now filled the air.

Several pots of coffee and plates of croissants later, we would emerge into the sunshine to continue the most urgent project at the time: the creation of three self-contained apartments from the damp, grey, concrete shells which Gary had abandoned as his legacy.

The men worked quickly. There was no more carping about millimetres and perfect finishes. No judgements, silly competitive comparisons, or puerile points to be scored in order to bolster the inadequacy of insecure individuals. This was a mountain home, we had always wanted it to be built in the rustic style typical of local construction, and these chaps now understood me, and respected my decisions and wishes. In return, I respected their talents and experiences in various areas, and we worked together smoothly as a team, each of us infusing a little of himself into the finishing of the walls, floors and ceilings. If any of us needed help or advice, we would discuss the potential solutions together, never being made to feel ignorant or small for requiring assistance. Things thus moved on a lot faster, in a vastly improved atmosphere, and the days passed quickly.

We had already received a call from England to the effect that an old client of mine from art gallery days, Martin, a traffic policeman, along with his wife and their friend, intended to be our first paying customers once we were ready to open for business. When, he had asked me, would the apartments be available to rent? We gave him a date in August which would be convenient for his summer holiday, not wishing to lose the first income we would receive since the sale of the gallery way back in December 2002.

That gave us just twelve weeks to achieve our goal. Twelve weeks in which to install floors, interior walls, ceilings, windows, doors, electricity, plumbing, furniture, kitchenettes and, of course, a means of descending the slippery slope from the parking area to the house and apartments below. The three apartments covered a total area of a hundred and eighty square metres, the size of a reasonably large house, and it certainly looked as though the summer was going to involve a huge and concerted effort from all those helping us to reach the target.

Tony added pigment to plaster to save painting time later, he demonstrated a method of creating false stone flooring by colouring white cement and carving "joints" into the surface as it dried, and he taught us a plastering technique which took half the time of that before. He even engraved oriental murals into the drying walls to create his own, unique finish. Along with the application and adaptability of young Baptiste, we made good progress.

As Tony battled on with the vast areas that needed to be plastered, Jean-Luc and Big Phil rejoined us for the installation of three independent plumbing systems, while Baptiste and I put in place the conduits and plug points for the electrical systems. We contacted Peter once again – the tall, quiet Englishman who had completed the wiring professionally for us in the upper part of the house – and he agreed to return to repeat the process for the three apartments.

One day, as I assisted him by pulling the individual cables through their respective protective conduits, he expressed doubt as to whether we would have enough electricity to supply all our needs. We had been forced, due to financial constrictions, to abandon hopes of an oil-fired heating system in favour of wall-mounted, electrical heaters, which were cheap to buy and quickly fitted. He informed me that the temporary supply provided by the electricity company was intended for building site use only, and could not be boosted to cover all our needs on three floors until after the final installation of a new post, meter and cabling on to our land. (At the time, our provisional supply was drawn through a site meter, via a heavy cable swung between the trees that lined the highway, from the nearest neighbour's post, some hundred and fifty metres up the road.) He told us that at the present level of power, there was a risk of the current being tripped at the meter if our house and all three apartments were to overload the system: for example, if all heaters and kitchens were being used simultaneously, or if all four water heating boilers were to switch on together. At the time, such huge demands on our electricity supply seemed a remote risk, and besides, I felt sure we would have our new post and personal meter fully in place in the weeks ahead. Never had I been so wrong.

Peter finished his work, and I applied to the electricity board for our definitive house supply and meter. Several weeks and numerous telephone calls later, a huge wad of contractual paperwork arrived, containing also a diagram showing the planned positions of the posts along the road which would be necessary to carry our new supply.

It was apparently up to us to find out from the local *mairie* who owned the land adjacent to ours on which, so I surmised at the time, a post would have to be erected in order to carry the final cable from the nearest source to the top of our drive. Once I had informed them of the proprietor's details, the electricity company would make application to the owner for permission of the installation of said post on the fringe of their land, even though it was just a metre from the side of the road. It was all becoming somewhat long-winded.

Of course, the *mairie* was closed as I arrived, as they had just decided that, having changed the opening hours three times during the last month, another alteration would not go amiss. The following day, however, there was someone there who was able to help me, and duly informed me of the name and address of the proprietor of the problematic parcel of land lying between us and eventual electrical fulfilment.

It turned out to be a middle-aged lady who was not only a resident of a town an hour's drive distant, but also, we heard, spent half the year holidaying in America! And our electricity supply proper could not be installed until we had her written permission for the use of a square foot of land bordering the road. The clammy grip of frustration began once again to constrict us within its gnarled, confining fingers.

Chapter 28

Finding the lady's name and current address had not been a problem; making contact, however, was another thing entirely. I despatched the relevant paperwork requiring her signed permission for the erection of the post, and attempted to follow it up with a friendly chat, during which I hoped to help her understand the need to finalise our electrical supply. After several weeks, I began to tire of the message on her answerphone, and made the journey to her hometown in a desperate bid to actually communicate with the woman and thus conclude this irritating episode in the construction chronicle. Finding her house locked and silent, I posted a note through her letterbox to the effect that we had called and found her absent, and drove home, dispirited.

I tried to mentally shelve the non-resolution of the electrical problem, as it was not actually hindering progress elsewhere. However, because the site supply was being charged at a rate higher than the normal domestic tariff, it niggled at me constantly as we worked towards the completion of the apartments.

An amusing distraction during the summer was provided when our friend Bob Drury, a professional paraglider pilot resident in Cipières, was approached by the BBC to assist them with a documentary based around the migrational habits of bar-headed geese. The producers needed footage of some birds flying against a mountain landscape in order to portray the geese on their traditional flight across the Himalayas from northern India. To accomplish this, they decided to use Bob's flying skills to train some young birds to follow him in the air, so that, when filmed against the hills of the Alpes-Maritimes, it would appear to the viewers that the birds were genuinely being followed by the camera across the world's highest mountain range.

Bob flew a paraglider fitted with a motor for the exercise, a device facilitating the ability to launch from a level field and climb into the air without having to depend upon thermic updraughts in the normal way.

The paramotor also allowed Bob to fly at greater airspeeds than were usually possible, so that he would be able to lead the young gaggle as they were trained to follow him.

It was an amusingly bizarre sight to behold indeed. Most mornings, over the course of several months, Bob would arrive on the local landing field in the village with the birds and his flying equipment in a windowless van; the geese would be kept in the dark while Bob arranged his gear on the field and prepared for take-off. He would then launch his glider and, at the appropriate moment, the geese would be released as he flew past the opening doors. Since birth, the geese had come to see this unwieldy conglomeration of nylon, propeller and human being as their mother, and would brainlessly lob themselves into the air behind it as soon as they saw it flying before them.

There were some hilarious moments. On one occasion, we watched enthralled as Bob buzzed past the van, the doors were opened, and the geese threw themselves after him. All went well until Bob initiated a sharp turn, at which point the geese continued obliviously in a straight line; his irritation being audibly broadcast over the radio to his assistants, and anyone within a hundred-metre radius, on the ground:

'Oh, no!' he screamed for all the world to hear, 'I've lost the fucking geese again!' as the now distant gaggle disappeared into the far reaches of the valley.

Towards the end of the summer, however, they came to follow the machine more consistently, but a looming threat was provided by the imminent arrival of the hunting season. Bob intensified his efforts, and the birds were finally trained to an acceptable level just two days before they risked being shot out of the sky by any number of eager village hotshots.

The film was successfully broadcast later in the year. Few people watching could have possibly imagined the peculiarly droll nature of its creation.

As the heat of summer days transformed the world into a kaleidoscopic cauldron of colour, brimming with life and light, the house finally began to enter the terminal phases of its evolution. The vibrating beauty of the surrounding paradise seeped osmotically into our senses, and we were filled with a calm contentment despite the obstacles ahead.

Chapter 28

A major problem was posed by the total lack of any proper stairway linking either front or back entrances of the house to the parking area, which was situated on a higher terraced level. Everyone was still compelled to struggle their way up, or pick their way carefully down, a steep and rock-strewn incline which was responsible for several nasty grazes on the limbs of both adults and children alike during their attempts to navigate its hazards; unnerving enough when dry, terrifying when wet.

Tony suggested the use of old railway sleepers for the treads of a proper flight of steps: they were relatively cheap, far more attractive in a mountain setting than dull concrete and, due to their previous anti-rot treatment, would last for life. I was informed by various villagers that the first place to try was the old railway terminal at Grasse, which had recently been undergoing renovation. I was sure to find what I required there, they told me. Several confusing telephone calls, on the other hand, were to reveal once again that nothing was as straightforward as we always liked to hope. The modernisation work at Grasse had been finished, and any unused items, including lorryloads of old sleepers, had been transported to a depot in a town at least two hours' drive distant.

We spent a few days making enquiries as to the cost of hiring a truck (with accompanying driver holding an appropriate licence) which would be up to the task of transporting the considerable weight of thirty railway sleepers from their current resting place to Gréolières. The cost proved to be totally prohibitive. It appeared that we had encountered yet another brick wall across the path to success.

One lunchtime, we were enjoying some grilled fish which Big Phil had brought along to cook over a makeshift barbecue of concrete blocks and old steel bars, when the subject of the elusive sleepers happened to find its way into the midday banter.

'You need sleepers? Why didn't you say so before?' he asked, as if it was the work of but a moment to acquire what we needed.

'What! You mean you know where to source them, Phil?' I responded, amazed; we had made further, exhaustive enquiries to no avail.

'I know where to find anything you want, my friend,' came the reply, as he threw back his head and laughed at the sky. 'Yes, you need something, Phil can get it,' he continued, 'and you won't be waiting long!'

I told him we were going to want about thirty sleepers, which would be cut in half to form the sixty-odd treads for our garden stairway.

'Hmm, I can definitely get twenty, and by tomorrow, how about that?'

I was stunned. As I wrestled to resist asking the obvious questions, I envisaged in my mind's eye a comical scene in which Phil arrived the following day and unloaded the goods from off the back of a lorry. The following day, Phil arrived and unloaded the goods from off the back of a large white van, but the slight discrepancy in anecdotal vehicle type did nothing to prevent the smirk on my face as we neatly stacked the sleepers under a large rock, out of sight of quizzical passers by.

We finally had something with which to start our stairway, and I happily asked him how much he wanted for his work. He required two hundred euros, and reasonably agreed to be paid the next day as I had no cash at the house and could not, of course, use any other payment method. We decided to meet at Les Quatres Chemins, a well-known junction just south of Grasse city centre, and I duly turned up and waited for the man at the designated spot.

Situated on the roundabout was a large fast-food restaurant, adorned in yellow and red: I thought of good old Ron and the desperate days we had experienced together as I waited for my new friend to arrive. I sincerely hoped Ron had been able to carve out some sort of satisfactory existence for his little family since those troubled times.

My musings were interrupted by the machine-gun sound of a Second World War fighter plane plummeting pell-mell from the sky, or so it seemed. As the noise became almost unbearable, Phil swooped into view atop the lowest-slung, loudest, fattest and blackest Harley Davidson I had ever seen. He roared to a stop beside me, opened his arms and hugged me in greeting, looking for all the world like the bastard offspring of a female gorilla and the lead singer of ZZ Top.

He asked me if I had the family in tow, and I responded in the negative.

'Well, hey! Then I'll take you to my locale! Get on the back!'

'But, Phil,' I said slowly, surveying the "hardtail" nature of the rear of the bike and the huge metal mudguard behind his single perch, 'there's no seat.'

'What are you: some kind of pussy?' he countered. 'Get on the bike, you great pansy!'

As I slung my short leg over the broad guard with all the grace of an arthritic pot-bellied pig, I suddenly realised I had no helmet, which I presumed was compulsory in France as in England.

'Er, Phil,' I shouted above the deafening din of the huge engine, 'what's the score here with helmets? What's the law on that one?'

In his inimitable way, he threw back his head and roared with laughter.

'Law? What law? Ben, this is my town!' he happily retorted, opening up the throttle and nearly dumping me in the road as the muscular machine rocketed off up the street, swerving like a slalom skier around parked cars and traffic islands along the way.

I had ridden motorbikes on and off for twenty-three years, but nothing I had learned in that time could have prepared me for that short, shocking, surreal experience. I was frantically clinging to the sharp underside of a rounded mudguard, every bump and jolt from the road resonating from my tortured coccyx to the base of my brain, while the sensual sensation of the city wind in (what remained of) my hair and the satisfyingly powerful throbbing of the hefty motor beneath us offered an impression of liberty and freedom I had long forgotten. Like a Valkyrie exploding from Valhalla, Phil was oblivious to speed limits as we screamed through the suburban streets, passing police who playfully saluted from their patrol cars as we blasted past them. Phil was Ogri, and the scene was the strip-cartoon of a biker's fantasy.

Through an industrial estate, over a piece of waste ground and skidding to a halt behind a disused warehouse, Phil finally brought the exhilarating rocket-ride to an end. I dismounted, standing for several seconds with orangutan legs as I contemplated our new surroundings.

We had parked outside a low, dark building, whose barred doors suggested something sinister or precious lurking within. Across the lintel, in a sweeping arc, was a sign bearing the ominous words "BANDIDOS de France" in red and yellow lettering. From somewhere unseen came the stomach-churning howl of a monstrous animal: I experienced a little of the terror so graphically portrayed by Conan Doyle in *The Hound of the Baskervilles.* Phil assured me that the dog was chained, and proceeded to unlock a seemingly endless series of locks, grilles and metal shutters which formed a many-layered barrier to anyone stupid enough to attempt a forced entry.

Freeing the final padlock, Phil opened a heavy wooden door and ushered me into the gloomy interior of his private sanctuary. There was but one small window, giving on to a walled yard in which the dog was kept, but the rest of the light was artificial, illuminating a vast room whose walls were painted a predictable matt black, and hung with an array of framed photographs charting the club's history from time immemorial, or so it appeared. There was a snooker table, televisions, a shower room off to one side, and sofas which became beds as and when required. Facing us as we entered was a bar running the entire length of the opposite wall, and it was to here that I was now directed.

'You have the money?' Phil asked, as he walked round the bar to face me.

'Of course,' I replied, and laid the notes on the bar.

'My friend! You are to be trusted! Thank you. You are now my guest,' he said.

With a collusive smile playing upon his lips, he opened the fridge beside him and grabbed two handfuls of the small beers which for some reason or other are the norm in Europe, and slammed two or three of the little bottles down on the bar in front of me.

'Here is my number,' he said, as he handed me a small card. 'Never hesitate to call if you need help. Give it to your lovely wife, also. You are always welcome here. Just say you are Phil's friend.'

We spent half an hour discussing things diverse, and I was instructed in the history of the Bandidos.

'Sort of French Hell's Angels, then?' I conjectured. Bad mistake.

'What?! Fucking Hell's Angels?! Ha! We eat them for breakfast! We spit in their face! They are nothing to us!'

Yes, I thought, and their mothers were hamsters and their fathers smelt of elderberries, Phil, but I love you and your friendship nonetheless.

Priceless.

Chapter 29

As if problems with the electricity supply, the health service (we had been exchanging letters for months in a so-far unsuccessful bid to become integrated into the state healthcare system – the difficulty being that we were technically self-employed yet had no income), and various financial institutions were not enough, the simple installation of a telephone line in our new home proved to be equally arduous.

In an attempt to thwart the problems posed by a completely new telephone number, I had called France Telecom before leaving the village apartment. I was assured that, once established in the new house, it would be absolutely no problem whatsoever to continue the existing contract at a new address. Our six weeks ensconced in a caravan, however, seemed to have put the cat of confusion amongst the Telecom pigeons. After several further weeks of non-communication with the outside world – during which time we either shamefacedly borrowed the house phones of our friends, or, with teeth gritted against its disproportionately inflated charges, used our recently-acquired mobile – we had still not been connected at the house.

A trip to Grasse and an appointment at the telephone company's offices were required to finally get things under way. It transpired that they had been waiting for the installation of a new pole by the electricity people, which they themselves would use in a crafty cost-cutting exercise. But, of course, that pole could not be installed until we had contacted a certain elusive landowner for permission to erect the other one further up the road!

Maybe the maniacal grimace resulting from the intense frustration I felt within had some sort of effect upon the employee seated before us, for he spontaneously agreed to install the new line, with the old number, within the next week. To accomplish this, they would be using me to dig a trench alongside the road and lay a fat, green, flexible conduit to carry the cable from our property to a neighbour's telegraph pole some forty metres away. It really seemed that they wanted to avoid the expense of an additional pole at all costs. I returned home in better mood and set to work to lay the caterpillar-like tubing. Job done, I called France Telecom in order that they could now, at last, come and make the definitive connection.

When the men in blue finally arrived a few days later to install our line, it looked as though at least one piece of the utilities jigsaw was finally fitting into place. Until, that is, we attempted to make our first call. While the other party could hear us perfectly clearly, their voice was not only muffled, but accompanied by what sounded like frying bacon, a swarm of hornets and an eighteenth-century elephant hunt.

It was to be a further ten days before we eventually obtained a normal telephone service in our new residence.

One of the final jobs to complete before August and the arrival of our first guests was to apply the façade to the exterior of the walls of the house. Although internally everything was now almost functional, the grey concrete blocks presented a rather ugly face to the world.

Tony informed me that he had done the job before, by hand, applying a mixture of white cement and sharp sand using a simple hand-trowel, although ours would be his biggest project to date, the walls having a surface area of over three hundred square metres. The only difficulty was the problem of scaffolding the house, which was surrounded on all sides by uncompromisingly uneven, rocky ground. In addition, the amount required would be enormous, and thus extremely expensive to hire.

One day, as I was descending from the village to the *prefecture* at Nice to replace my residence permit – which, with the help of some small child or other, had found its way into the domestic rubbish bin and subsequently the village garbage along with the rest of the community's debris – I spied a ramshackle scaffolding system beside the house of Jacqui, the iron worker, and dropped by to ask if we could possibly borrow it. Grinning from ear to ear, the man laughed as he told me that of course I could borrow it, as long as I dismantled it and replaced it in the same position once we had finished with it.

I took the agile Baptiste along with me the following day, and spent a terrifying hour or so upon the trembling structure as we took it apart from the top down. It was then that I understood the mirth of its owner; it was obviously a job he would rather not have attempted himself. It took three trips in our old people carrier to transport all the aging poles and brackets, and a whole day to erect the framework against the first wall of the house to be treated.

With Tony and Baptiste perched precariously aloft, it became my job to produce the sticky, sandy *mélange* in the cement mixer, then hoist it up to where they were working, utilising an old climbing rope, a pulley and several buckets. I began to understand the skill of the campanologist as I attempted to remain on the ground while the heavy buckets flew up and down. We had noticed small birds nesting in the holes in the irregularities of the walls; we did our best to ensure they had been evacuated before being interred in miniature concrete tombs.

After two weeks, the façade was finished, leaving three exhausted workers with biceps like cannon balls. It was a cathartic moment indeed. The house, clothed in its new shade of textured beige, finally melded into the surrounding environment like the others in the area, and appeared as though it had always been there.

In the middle of August, with the Bandidos' steps in place, and the furnishing of the apartments having been accomplished by the spectacular shopping skills of Karen, we celebrated with champagne at our second summer village ball.

We were ready to receive our first guests.

Chapter 30

Just a few days before our friend Martin, his wife Sue, and friend Judith descended upon us from flatland Norfolk, we were surprised, one warm evening, to hear the sound of motorcycle engines roaring into the driveway above the house. I stepped out on to the terrace to witness the most amazing display of multiple formation parking imaginable. Six similar bikes skidded to a halt in neat herringbone configuration, from which alighted six identically-clad, unfeasibly tall figures of similar height, in black leather. I thought German, then Swiss. No other nation on earth could produce such mind-numbingly regular repetition of bike-style, clothing and dull neatness of parking. Stiff as a cock in the morning.

Each clasping his matching matt-black helmet to his side, they descended the newly-laid steps to the house. In a thick Germanic accent, one of them asked whether we had accommodation available for the night.

'Er, yeah, no problem,' I answered, my mind working on the possible arrangements of single beds available to house such large, powerful bodies. 'There are three apartments; all free at the moment. As we charge a rate per person per night, rather than for the apartment itself, and you're all big guys, why not spread yourself out and have plenty of room?' I was glad to be able to offer them the space I thought they needed.

'Oh, no,' the huge, handsome, muscular chap responded, 'vee vould like to be togezzer ...!'

Exclaiming thus, he winked at me and camply tossed his blond head towards his compatriots.

'Right, excellent, no problem!' I responded, amused at the thought of six bulky blokes christening our enterprise, and relieved that, even if messy, we would at least be cleaning only one of the apartments the following morning.

On the Saturday of the same week, we attended, *en famille*, the wedding of Jean-Luc, our plumber. We had become good friends during the period in which he had been working for us, and it had been gratifying to receive the invitation to his marriage in Grasse.

I had sworn never to wear a suit again, but I hypocritically succumbed to the pressures of convention and dug out an old black number from the bottom of a large cardboard box which had remained sealed since the day we left England and had incarcerated all such frivolous garb in a Norwich side-street garage.

The wedding was conducted in a quaint, medieval chapel which, in turn, formed part of an imposing historic building alongside the cathedral itself. We arrived with time to spare, and spent twenty minutes or so surveying the interior of the cathedral, whose walls were adorned with three huge canvases by Rubens. Although I had left the commercial art world for good, it was a precious moment when I finally viewed these masterpieces; the beauty of art far transcends any monetary value that one can ever hope to put on it.

Commenting on its aesthetic value, which in his eyes was far more important than any practical application, Oscar Wilde once said, "All art is quite useless." Indeed, old chap, and life would be quite useless without it.

Jean-Luc was obviously an exceptionally popular fellow. Friends and relations simply swarmed into the mayor's building over the next quarter of an hour, like so many ten-year-old girls to a concert by the latest boy band. The little chapel accommodated only a small proportion of those present, and we found ourselves watching from beyond the open doorway as the happy couple prepared themselves for the ultimate commitment.

It be a strange thing, marriage. Centuries of religious tradition have led us to believe that it is the natural situation in which to find oneself as an adult. And yet centuries of fornication, whoring, affairs and deceit have not, for some reason, convinced us that it is probably at best flawed, or at worst, a ridiculous institution serving only the purposes of political, commercial and religious leaders, who require their underlings to conform to a set pattern so as to further their own interests in power gains, wealth development or social control.

We all know that the two sexes originated from different planets and we all know that we find each other not only difficult to understand, but often impossible to share a space with, and yet we still insist on rearing children to believe it is normal and correct to hold that there is only one special person out there. And when found, this person must be jealously guarded and controlled in a catastrophic collapse of the individual who once was, to become a domesticated cog in the grindingly boring gearbox of existence.

We are incredibly different as animals, and I do believe that it is impossible to force the opposite sex into seeing things as we do.

Having struggled with such issues for many years, I am convinced that, as humans, we are just not being honest with ourselves at an intimate level. Why, for example, does pornography exist? Why is there always work for prostitutes? Why do both men and women enjoy sexual fantasising, whether realised or not? If we have evolved to be with one sexual partner for life then surely such things would not exist to the extent that they do; and definitely not for those with a current partner, either in our heads as ideas, or as physical representations of those thoughts that lurk constantly in the recesses of our minds. It was the writings of Desmond Morris that first awakened me to the evident possibility that perhaps the lives we lead are rather more unnatural than either religious or political interest would want us to believe.

As the human animal evolved as a sexually-reproductive organism, then two distinct types of the creature became extant. We could call them male and female, yin and yang, or anything else you care to, but, right from the start, both were essential to reproduce the species; and both were equally important and necessary in the further development of knowledge and understanding of the world in which they found themselves.

There is no room here for mindless, sexist poppycock. We are obviously as valid as each other, and dependent on each other for everything that the other half of the population does better than we do. My argument comes from the standpoint that we will only survive as a species if we love and respect our fellow man or woman, and strive towards a future of peace in the world. And we will only make progress in our personal relationships if, instead of knee-jerk reactions to the behaviour of the opposite sex, we sit down and communicate openly with each other as to the reasons and motivations for the behaviour that our partner finds intolerable. For example, rather than walking into the local branch of W.H. Smith and ripping the top shelf apart in a yobbish display of misunderstanding, it would be far more constructive to actually ask why men, and, in my experience, a lot of women, enjoy looking at erotica. Instead of reacting to the symptoms, why on earth can we not investigate the cause? One does not solve the problem of a collapsing house by renewing the wallpaper.

It has been suggested that, as type A human developed more physical strength along with the lifelong ability to fertilise the other, type B correspondingly developed powers of communication and persuasion in order to control and complement their counterpart. If a fine, strong male specimen impregnated a particularly intelligent female, then the result would be powerful offspring who stood a better chance of survival than most of their contemporaries. Then the female in turn, lacking the muscular force to impose her will over the other, would naturally develop emotional and communicative techniques in order to persuade the male to stay with her and produce more of the same, rather than dashing off and impregnating another partner, according to his instinct. This would explain, perhaps, why a woman, who is deeply in love with and attracted to a particular man, feels no need to cast an eye towards other, physically attractive men who pass her way. Her inherited instinct is usually to preserve and protect that which provides strong and intelligent offspring on repeated occasions.

On the other hand, a man who is in love with and sexually attracted to a particular woman, will still be distracted by other females of striking appearance or pleasing personality; the cause of which harks back to the evolutionary necessity to propagate the species for as long as he lives. I would even go so far as to suggest that a man can be genuinely in love with more than one woman at a time, without diminishing the love he feels for any one of them. But, of course, our society has been built along different parameters of acceptance, and he is therefore compelled to play the role of monogamy, desperately seeking sad sexual outlets through the channels of prostitution and/or pornography. Even though many men play the game demanded of them outwardly, afraid to give voice to that which has lurked within since time immemorial, it has to be said that it is as difficult for a man to accept the concept of one sexual partner for life as it is for a woman to feel unbothered by the thought of her partner fucking another woman. And there it is.

There is no absolute resolution to the problem. Hopefully, couples will strive to communicate freely, forming stronger ties of love and friendship through the processes of honesty and through the trust that whatever comes to pass, they will always have the security provided by the proximity of someone who truly loves them.

A final note: chimpanzees have testicles the size of oranges, and impregnate several hundred females during their lifetime. Gorillas have testicles the size of peas, and impregnate four or five females during their active years. The size of a man's testicles is roughly halfway between the two.

Just as Jean-Luc and his lady rose to take the vows of betrothal, a deafening mechanical roar from the courtyard below the open window demolished all possibility of anyone hearing anything at all, and a smile crept across Jean-Luc's face as he paused, waiting for his friend to be present to witness the final capitulation.

We had never seen Phil dressed in anything but his Bandidos t-shirt and leather dungarees, but Karen had assured me that, for his friend's wedding, he would "make an effort" and present himself more conservatively attired. I had expressed a doubt, and we laughed openly as a hot, sweaty Phil, adorned in his regulation yellow and tan, bounded up the stairs to witness his friend's marriage; chest heaving as he beamed radiantly to the throng assembled.

The wedding ceremony having been completed, all present meandered a hundred yards from the official building into a sizzling, summer-scented courtyard, surrounded on three sides by imposing medieval architecture. The fourth boundary was provided by a low, stone wall, over which one could behold the panoramic vista of the lower levels of the city, then the green-swathed hillocks of the plain beyond, as it spread out and on towards the coast, the warm Mediterranean sparkling and twinkling in the distant haze.

Champagne was served, then wine, and it was a merry crowd that departed for the reception proper, which had been professionally organised at the home of Jean-Luc and his new bride, a few kilometres out of town.

My comprehension of spoken French at that time was somewhat inferior to the sentences I was able to verbalise, and we were confused as to the best route to take in order to arrive at the house for the celebration. Having made several unsuccessful attempts to understand exactly where it was that we were supposed to be going, Phil clapped a large hand across my shoulders and offered to lead the way on his motorbike.

My recent experience of Phil's biking behaviour left me with some doubt as to whether we could possibly keep up with him on the busy, archaic road system of the old town, but our fears were short-lived. He rode slowly, and with panache, constantly checking his mirrors to ensure that we were following behind. As we approached an extremely busy, but extremely small, roundabout, we were treated to an unbelievable spontaneous gesture of masterful care and control by the big man taking the lead. While cars hurtled on to, round and across the dustbin-lid junction, Phil and his monster machine eased forwards and halted in the middle of the now constipated highway. Calmly dismounting, the huge man held up his hands to the incoming tide of traffic, which slowed and obeyed his command, in much the same way that for King Canute, the sea did not. We were aghast. As Phil brought the world to a standstill before our very eyes, he turned, winked, and waved us through the breach he had just created.

Repeating the same display of magnanimous manipulation at two further points along the route, Big Phil escorted us finally to the house of his friend, where we celebrated life, love and friendship into the early hours.

Chapter 31

At the end of August – on the same day that Francesca found herself face-to-face with an enormous wild boar in the middle of the driveway, which stood stock still until she had retreated, in shocked terror, back to the house – we received our first group booking from a paragliding school in Dorset.

I had met the school's flying instructor, Andrew, a year or so earlier in La Barricade, and had been drawn to his gentle character. We had been in the early stages of building at the time, but he had taken our details, and now, true to his word, was about to bring twelve newly-qualified pilots to stay in the three apartments below the house. This was the sort of business we had always hoped would come our way, based on our connections within the paragliding community.

If it had not been for my learning to fly myself, years before on the windswept hills of the Peak District, then I doubt that the series of occurrences that ultimately led us to embark on the greatest adventure of our lives would have happened at all.

I had formerly been a keen rock climber, although my squat, stocky stature prevented my attaining any levels of real competence. I remember struggling halfway up a particularly featureless piece of rock once, on Stanage Edge, and shouting down to those amused by my unsightly contortions below:

'I can't reach the next handhold!'

'Climb up to it then,' came the facetious response.

As I battled upwards, wondering why on earth I had been born with an unfeasible compunction to push myself beyond that which is necessary for a comfortable existence, a shadow in the form of a huge, horizontally-inverted banana floated across the rock face, and I glanced skywards. Spellbound, I stared at its source. A gigantic kite was flying overhead, slung beneath which was a middle-aged chap, seated in the most relaxed manner imaginable, calmly waving down to me as his craft sailed silently by, maintaining its altitude above the ridge.

I knew at once that, rather than clinging to a vertical rock wall by my fingertips, I wanted to find out how to fly. And thus was born the passion that would change my world.

I recalled summer days on the school playing field as a child of eight years old, lying on my back with my hands clasped behind my head, transfixed by the movements of the clouds in the blue infinity above. As I watched their formation and dissolution, I longed to be up there, far from the torrid turmoil of earthbound existence, lost in a magic world of air and weightless flight. Paragliding provided the final fulfilment of the childhood fantasy. To take a rucksack from your back, and five minutes later be rendered airborne by its contents, is the most surreal experience conceivable. The first time my feet left the floor, as I sensed the mighty power of the wind pulling me bodily into the air, I knew that this was not going to be some passing interest, but the obsession of a lifetime. There are simply no words to describe the sharply elevated levels of consciousness one experiences during the departure of terra firma by the simplest form of free flight in existence.

I learnt how to seek out the thermals – the columns of rising air which carry the birds aloft – and with some experience, remain in the sky for hours at a time. To soar the majestic ridges of the mountain uplands, to fly alongside eagles, to leave the trivia of life's daily routine on the ground while the spirit flies freely in the heavens: this is paragliding.

It is, as they say, the most exciting thing you can do with your clothes on; although there are times when I believe it is better even than that.

Early September was a difficult time for Karen. Carrying her fourth, and our third, child throughout the long heat of the southern summer had taken its toll on her endurance, and she was looking forward to the end of it all with impatience. After all, young Tom was only just over a year old and, adorable though he was, with his headful of tumbling yellow curls and mischievous smirk, it seemed to my long-suffering wife that she had been pregnant for years.

Following the traumatic, drawn-out affair that had accompanied Tom's arrival, she was more than a little nervous as the estimated time of delivery drew nearer, tentatively pencilled-in for the twenty-first of September.

Chapter 31

The heavy days of laborious expectation finally drew to a close, and each morning I checked the fuel level in the car. The hospital in Grasse was a good hour's drive away and I didn't fancy the task of delivering my own child on the floor of the vehicle, marooned on a lonely mountain road due to lack of attention to minor details during the final days of Karen's pregnancy.

On the evening of the twentieth, however, as I drove home from the small supermarket at the other end of the village, my eye was caught by the sudden downward movement of the fuel gauge needle.

I had owned many cars since passing my driving test some twenty-four years earlier, but never had the playful pixie of the dashboard chosen a worse moment to tinker with indicated fuel levels. I swallowed hard, but felt comforted to remember that none of my children had ever actually arrived on the prescribed day. I made a mental note to top up the petrol in the morning, and retired to bed without giving the matter a second thought.

At five o'clock in the morning, I was awoken gently by Karen, who informed me that something was happening.

'Mmm ...?'

'Ben!' she whispered hoarsely, so as to prevent waking the other members of the household, 'I think my contractions have started!'

'What?!' Nothing had ever roused me so fast. 'OK, let me know when they are about a quarter of an hour apart, and we'll leave for the hospital.'

'They're closer than that already. About seven minutes. I wanted to make sure; I didn't want to wake you unnecessarily.'

I almost had a heart attack thanks to her thoughtfulness.

'Seven minutes?! Right, tea, quick, let's sort Sophie out.'

Our friend Sophie had offered to sit for Francesca, Emily and Thomas at the critical moment, so Karen rang her number as I prepared some fortifying tea for the pair of us. There was no reply.

Shit. Contractions coming regularly at seven minutes, the hospital an hour away through the blackness of early morning – and reached by some of the loneliest roads in the region – and now no one to look after the children. What on earth were we going to do? It was then that I remembered the petrol. I bit my lip and said nothing.

Shaking Francesca awake, a difficult enough business at normal hours of the day, we packed her off, bleary-eyed, to the village house where Sophie lived, while I stayed with Karen, preparing myself for any eventuality that could possibly arise. I knew that Josie, the owner of La Barricade, had delivered at least two babies on the floor of her restaurant in days gone by, and I steeled myself to call on her expertise if required. Twenty minutes later, however, Francesca returned with a panting Sophie. It appeared that the phone simply hadn't been sufficiently loud enough to wake her up, but all was now well, and with Sophie getting into our large bed with little Tom who needed a reassuring cuddle, Karen and I walked up to the waiting car as fast as it seemed safe to do so. I settled her down on the back seat and set off down the dark mountain roads. Never had Grasse seemed so far away.

After ten minutes of the journey had passed, and we entered the dank depths of the Gorges du Loup, a particularly cold place at that time of the morning, the fuel warning light decided that then would be the most appropriate time to illuminate. I hoped that Karen would not be able to see the reflection of its sinister orange glow in the plastic fascia of the dashboard, and tried to calculate how far we still had left to go. It would be about fourteen miles. Fourteen miles of sheer terror as far as I was concerned. I asked Karen to let me know when each contraction started, so I could get an idea of how things were progressing, and I checked the intervals against the time indicated on our mobile phone.

Six minutes. Gulp.

'Don't worry, love! Still seven minutes. We'll get there in time!'

Five minutes. And running on vapours.

'How long now, Ben? It's feeling close. Is there far to go?'

Four and a half minutes. Oh, fuck.

'You're fine, love,' I lied. 'Still nearly seven minutes apart. And we'll be at the hospital in ten minutes. Take it easy. It's all going to be alright.'

There was a good twenty minutes and nine miles of tortuous roads ahead, with no petrol station between us and the hospital which would be open at that hour. The longest twenty minutes of my life dragged its heels but eventually brought us to the long downhill stretch at the end of which the hospital was situated. Karen's contractions were now only a couple of minutes apart, but as I coasted into the car park with the car spluttering on the final drops of fuel, I finally knew for certain that, close though it had been, I would not be actually delivering my own child that morning.

We were received with startling efficiency and led to a small, comfortable chamber by a friendly midwife. Karen had indicated to me that she wanted me to explain to those present that her previous birth had been intolerably painful, and that on this occasion she wanted to be given some chemical help as soon as she found the process becoming too stressful. We had only been in the delivery room for fifteen minutes when the individual contractions became a continuous, involuntary pushing, and her face contorted in tense distress.

'Ben. Tell them I need something to kill the pain. I can't go through that again,' she begged me, squeezing my hand tightly as I stood helplessly beside her.

I explained to the midwife that it was all becoming too harrowing for Karen, and asked whether they would be good enough to administer some drugs for the pain. They answered in the negative.

'Oh, no!' Karen was almost weeping as the memory of her excruciating experience in a Norwich hospital flooded back to haunt her.

Like a repeated nightmare from which one is unable to rouse oneself, it appeared that she was beginning the horrible, agonizing ordeal all over again. She shouted through the pain.

'Ben! Ben! I can't cope! They don't understand! I can't do it without help this time! Please, please, oh, God!'

I appealed to the woman on Karen's behalf.

'Please. She really doesn't think she can do it unaided. Can you please give her something?'

'No, monsieur.'

'But why?' I implored.

'Because, monsieur, the baby's head is appearing! We can't administer drugs at this stage. Look!'

'What did she say? Hey?' Karen winced at me.

'She said you can't have any drugs because, guess what? The baby's being born!'

'Wha–? Already?!'

Her relief was palpable. Seconds later, following the most straightforward, natural birth I'd ever had the pleasure to witness, our new baby daughter made her entrance as Mum and Dad, the tears of shared wonder in their eyes, elatedly celebrated the miracle of new life.

We had entered the hospital at 7.30 a.m. Our new child had been born half an hour later.

After a further two hours, having ascertained that all was fine and normal, I left both of them to recover in the capable hands of the midwife, and headed for home to relieve Sophie of her baby-sitting duties. Halfway back up the gorge, I was taken aback as a huge black motorbike roared past the car and braked a short distance in front of me. I began to curse the idiocy of this apparent lunatic, when the black helmet was whisked from the head of Big Phil, and a grinning, hairy face lowered itself to the car window. He leaned through and planted a kiss on each of my cheeks.

'Ben! I thought it was you! I was in the bar back there and saw you go past. Fancy a drink?'

'Love to, normally, Phil, but Karen's just had the baby, and ...' I was cut short by a wave of engulfing enthusiasm.

'Had the baby? Today? Well, we must celebrate. Follow me back to the bar!'

I had no chance to argue as he re-mounted his mammoth machine and turned back down the hill. I hesitated for a second, then, turning the car in the road, followed after him. Sophie had all day, and I deserved a drink after all.

Chapter 32

French law requires the birth of a new baby to be registered within three days of its occurrence. We had not been able to decide on a name for our new little girl, and I procrastinated for a day or two before realising that, unless we made up our minds without further hesitation, we were going to exceed the allotted time span, leading to all sorts of paperwork difficulties relating to the French equivalent of "Family Allowance" and the like. On the third day after her arrival, I waltzed into the registry office in Grasse, an airy, wooden-panelled room situated in the same building in which Jean-Luc had been married just a few weeks earlier. An attractive, impeccably-attired clerk looked up from her desk.

'Monsieur Moss?' I was flabbergasted.

'Y ... yes, how did you know?'

'Your baby was born almost exactly three days ago. We have been expecting you. I'm glad you made it!'

I was amazed. It appeared that all documentation between the authorities was passed with the sort of efficiency rarely experienced in the United Kingdom. What I had not been aware of, however, was that the three days counted from the time of birth itself; and did not constitute three full days after the event as I had surmised. I was indeed fortunate to have chosen that moment to wander into the office. I had taken the opportunity to savour a beer or two in the little square around the corner before reporting in, and was now relieved that I had decided against a third, notwithstanding the balmy ambience of a late September afternoon.

While the clerk was creating the official forms to record the birth of our child, it suddenly occurred to me that the name we had finally chosen for her, Bonny, was also the name of a horse recently acquired by our friend Emily, with whom the family had briefly stayed during the five-week saga at the time of Tom's arrival fourteen months earlier. I smiled as I recalled the events surrounding the choice of the name "Emily" for our first child.

We had been invited to a folk festival by Emily and her partner Steve, which had taken place one hot August weekend in a springy, green Norfolk meadow. It was flanked on one side by a lazily-drifting river or canal, and on the other by a low, sprawling country pub, painted that hideous shade of pink that is, for some bizarre reason, slightly less repulsive when adorning the walls of thatched, period buildings. An ideal place indeed to while away a couple of days with good friends.

At the time, Karen and I had been courting for three years or so, and were content to be parenting her child Francesca, then seven, and my son Jo, fourteen, who lived with his mother for most of the week in her Norwich home. In addition, Matt and Hannah, my stepchildren from my first marriage and who were then in their early twenties, continued to play their own part in the multifarious world of my affections. Having become parents at the tender ages of twenty-four and twenty-one respectively, Karen and I had decided that we wanted no more offspring between us, thereby facilitating more time for our companions and interests as Francesca and Jo grew older and less dependent on their parents.

With Francesca away at a schoolmate's house for a day or two, we enjoyed a weekend of sun, music and laughter with our friends by the river, and felt a little dejected as we sat round the bonfire with Emily and Steve on the eve of our departure.

With enough good wine having been drunk throughout the long and sultry evening, Emily suddenly, and for no apparent reason, mentioned that she was able to divine the future from the reading of a person's palm. I laughed aloud. Ridiculous concept indeed. Karen, however, her spirits raised to a level of open-mindedness that I felt unable to share, moved round the fire to where Emily was sitting, and proffered her open hand. I smiled smugly, and concentrated on opening the next bottle of red. Emily, her swarthy complexion and long, hennaed tresses glowing gypsy-like as the flames danced before her handsome face, stared silently for a while at the upturned palm held in her own, and then gently placed the hand back in the lap of its owner.

'You're going to have another baby,' she said quietly, raising her glass to her mouth as she spoke.

'Ha!' I retaliated, disdainfully. 'That's not likely to happen in the foreseeable future!'

Karen, too, giggled at this preposterous prediction, while Emily smiled calmly, eyes aglow with fire and foresight.

I awoke early; the heat of the summer morning filled our little tent with an air of sweltering torpidity. Breathless, I threw the sticky sleeping bag aside, and was about to throw open the tentflap, when I suddenly halted, clapping eyes on the sleeping form of the woman beside me, who had apparently abandoned her own covering earlier in the night.

She was lying face down, her pretty face supported on linked hands beneath her cheek, but it was her body that riveted my attention and arrested further movement. The pale buttocks, twin orbs of delicious delight, rose to challenge my resolve, and I vacillated. A sexual compulsion rendered all the more inevitable by the dense weight and steamy heat of the atmosphere inside our clammy canvas cocoon overtook me, and I gently parted the hot legs of my partner. I lowered my burning body into hers, and she sighed gently as she awakened to the melting magic flowing between us.

Emily had predicted the conception of new life. Her prophesy had been fulfilled.

I was jolted from my reverie by the registry office clerk, who had processed the necessary documentation and was now presenting me with several free copies of a rather plain birth certificate. I enquired as to the reason for their number, and was politely told that there would be all sorts of situations ahead in which we, or Bonny herself when grown, would need a copy of the document. Logical; obvious even. Why doesn't this happen as a matter of course in England, I wondered?

It is often stated that there is a lot of paperwork involved with French bureaucracy and, from time to time, I would have to agree. On the other hand, the system is remarkably well-organised, as in the case of our monthly family allowance payment, which we began to receive soon after Bonny's birth. Assuming all paperwork has been completed and sent to the relevant bodies concerned, payments are automatically made without any further questioning or delays in the system. We even received one-off payments to assist with various other expenses, help which we hadn't actually been aware of, or solicited.

In contrast, I recalled valid social security claim situations in England in which one had to apply, reapply, fill in a new form when the office had lost it, be redirected to another part of the building, wait three months for one's application to be looked at, obtain all four grandparents' signatures in triplicate, and return from a voyage triumphantly waving the head of the Gorgon before even being considered for an interview to further the matter. I know where I'd rather be.

Karen was soon up and about again, although a little saddened to think she'd be losing the voluntary post she had been offered at the village school in Gréolières. Three months or so before the expected time of Bonny's birth, the hugely huggable headmistress Hélène, with whom we had shared wine-drenched evenings in La Pierre à Feu on more than one occasion, had asked Karen if she would mind assisting the children with the preparation of the end of term school play. Part of the production would involve children of around seven years of age singing a selection of English nursery rhymes along with their standard French tunes. Karen had jumped at the opportunity, especially as she was struggling with the language transition herself, and by interacting with the youngsters hoped to improve her grip on the indigenous tongue in exchange. She had been heavily pregnant at the time, but this presented no problem whatsoever to Hélène, a grandmother herself, and wildly popular with the children and parents alike.

Karen had smiled proudly during the sun-kissed performance in the playground at the end of June, as the local children's rendition of The Wheels on the Bus was sung flawlessly; albeit blessed with a lilting Provençal accent.

Now, however, with brand-new breastfed baby in tow, we presumed that the mutually-rewarding classroom experience would have to be curtailed for a while. Once again, we had underestimated the universal French acceptance of babies and children, this time even in the workplace. Hélène not only assured Karen that she wished her to continue with the informal English lessons, but also told her to bring the baby with her into the classroom, while she herself, the headmistress, would take the baby in her arms as and when Karen needed. Such unquestioning acceptance of new life as an integral and shared part of the community was a continuous, eye-opening experience for our family.

On one occasion, we called into our builders' merchant for some tool or other, Karen holding the gurgling bundle to her breast. We had, over the course of the previous year and a half, become well-known at the establishment, but I wasn't prepared for the reaction when they were confronted with baby Bonny for the first time. Receptionists came running from offices, butch young lads downed sacks of cement, and older, grizzled chaps flocked to see the new attraction, the whole place virtually coming to a standstill as one and all contested in their eagerness to hold, touch, kiss or cuddle our new child.

As a well-built, middle-aged fellow took the small baby in his arms, his warm smile radiating a gentle humanity rarely witnessed in equivalent male English circles, I was abruptly reminded of our old mechanic friend, Ian, greatly missed since the news of his untimely death the previous year. A few days before our return to France following the birth of Thomas, we had called into his garage to say our farewells for the second time.

Ian had never been so close to a baby and, being gay, was unlikely to have a child of his own. He regarded little Tom wistfully and, as we were about to leave, asked if he could hold him. Since he had not held a baby before, he explained, he would, for the first time in his life, like to enjoy the experience. Karen passed the two-week-old boy to the man, who gingerly held out his massive, muscular arms to receive the tiny person. Tom virtually fitted into just one of the big man's huge hands. Ian smiled at the child's face and, as we quietly regarded the muscle-bound colossus softening around the small, helpless human enfolded within his giant frame, we knew that we had been privileged to share in a very special moment.

It was the last we would ever see of the great man.

Chapter 33

Andrew and his pilots arrived at the beginning of October, and a more affable bunch of people it would be hard to imagine. They installed themselves in the three apartments, and all seemed tickety-boo until about twenty minutes after their arrival, when, out of the blue, the whole house was plunged into darkness. Here we were, with thirteen guests having just arrived, as Peter's dreaded, but long forgotten, electrical premonitions became frightening reality around us.

Coming to my senses, I scrambled upstairs to find a pair of shoes (shoes, candles and coats to hand would later become de rigueur), and ran madly from the house, hoping to reach the trip-switch up the road before anyone would really notice what was going on. The whole incident, between blackout and reinstatement of supply by a simple push of a button at the meter box, occupied perhaps three minutes, a duration we would endeavour to minimise during the weeks ahead. On my return, of course, it was necessary to turn off every electrical appliance in the house, to maximise the availability of power for our guests below, and to avert an immediate recurrence of the problem. Nevertheless, despite our best attempts at power-saving, the episode was to repeat itself on several more occasions over the next two weeks of their occupancy. I mentally vowed to up my efforts to contact the landowner lying between us and a normal, worry-free electricity supply.

Amongst the party of paraglider pilots staying with us on that occasion was a young woman of about twenty-five years old, who complained of restlessness during the first few nights of her stay. One dark evening, she surreptitiously approached me with an explanation of her predicament. It transpired that she found falling asleep difficult without partaking of the soporific services of cannabis, her dilemma being decidedly more pronounced when cramped into close quarters with a bunch of smelly, snoring, male paraglider pilots.

'Er, Ben,' she essayed, taking me aside on the terrace out of earshot of her compatriots, 'I think I'm safe in asking you this. You seem like a reasonable bloke … but obviously one doesn't want to cause offence ...'

'Take a lot to offend me,' I smiled. 'What's the prob?'

'Well, er, is there any way at all that one could get hold of some … mmm … hash around here? I mean, without causing any trouble?'

Ten minutes and one phone call later, my friend Pierre, the hunter, rolled up to join the party, large plastic bag in hand bearing his own home-grown speciality, and his lean, understanding face bearing a friendly grin.

There were several partakers that evening, following which any amount of snoring, farting and belching seemed to have been slept through quite blissfully.

Late in the month we were visited by two young journalists from Norwich, who arrived to spend several days with us with a view to compiling an article for the *Eastern Daily Press (EDP)*. Such article would be based around the madness of a couple who had deserted a comfortably secure life in a quaint, medieval English city in exchange for a wildly unpredictable existence on a remote French mountainside.

It wasn't the first time that this apparently bizarre move had attracted the attention of the media. Indeed, I had received a telephone call some four years earlier, while seated at my gallery desk in the gloomy twilight of a wet November afternoon.

'Hello. Could I speak to Ben Moss, please?'

For some reason, the satirical sprite in me always found it extraordinarily difficult, at times like this, not to affect the voice of another, responding with something along the lines of:

'Well, he's incredibly busy at present due to the huge popularity of the gallery here, but I'll do what I can for you, madam. Please bear with me while I ascertain whether or not he is in a position to be interrupted.'

I managed to resist the temptation of mischief on this occasion, however, and simply answered, 'Speaking.'

'Mr Moss, I represent Ricochet Productions for Channel Four. I've been given your name by Mr Goldsmith of Gréolières, in France. He tells me that you're planning to move out to that region in the foreseeable future?'

"Mr Goldsmith" was my friend Bruce, a paragliding guru whom I had first met in 1995, when I had flown over to participate in a training course for novice pilots based at his home in Le Bar-sur-Loup. This village was located about half an hour from Gréolières, to where he had later transferred his business and which had subsequently so appealed to my soul.

'Yes, that's right. Can I help you?'

'I certainly hope so! We're making a series of programmes around people who leave England to make like a new life in France, and we heard about Bruce; only he told us that he'd made the move several years ago. He recommended you since you're still at the like planning stages, which is exactly what we're looking for!'

'Go on,' I said, cautiously.

'When are you intending to relocate to France, Ben?' Oh, God. Christian-name journalese already.

'About a year from now, all being well. Why?'

'Could you tell us your plan, y'know, what you're going to like do there, etcetera?'

'We're going to sell everything we have here in order to fund the building of a house, with rooms to let, in Gréolières, and start a new life founded on the premise that less is more.'

'Fascinating! Great! Yes! We'd love to cover it. What do you say?'

I needed more to go on, as they say.

'Can you tell me exactly how this would work?' I asked. 'I mean, what do you want from us in plain terms?'

'OK, Ben, so you're off in about a year? That's the period during which we'd like to come and film you and your family in your home – to get like a background of your life before the adventure starts, yes, right? We also need to come and film your business, your friends, y'know … to get like an overall picture of your English life here. We'd then like follow the move, be there on site as you build the house, follow your progress, see the project through. Then, once everything's up and like running, maybe come and do some filming for a time afterwards, yeah? To complete the picture and show everyone how it's all going!'

'Right. Let's get this straight. You want free access to film me and my family at home now, over there, and afterwards, over a period of two years or so, yes?'

'You got it! Then we like take all the best bits, cut it down, and produce a documentary for television. What d'you say?'

'What's the fee?'

'Beg your pardon?'

'The fee. What do we get paid for the invasion of our privacy for two years? Unlimited access to stick cameras in our faces and the faces of our children and friends at home and at work for two years of our lives? You'll need an angle, of course. You'll need to play up babies screaming, couples arguing, plans gone wrong and all that stuff. Come on. What do we get for that sort of televisual rape?'

'Fee? Fee? What do you mean, fee? You'll be famous for forty minutes, Ben! Think of that! Famous! Your apartments will be filled for years to come! What d'you say?'

'Famous for forty minutes?! You're talking to the wrong person, my lovely. Apartments filled?!' I was spitting the words through jaws clenched tighter than a cokehead on Ecstasy. 'Once you lot have finished with us, no one within a million light years would want to set foot in our house! Now bog off!'

I was absolutely stupefied when the same girl rang me in France mid-way through the building process and tried again.

The reporters from the *EDP*, however, were coming to interview us in a virtually completed house, as our guests, and would hopefully tell the true story as we would tell it to them.

I met Shaun and Emma off the plane and escorted the cheerful young couple back to the village. The contrast in topography between flat Norfolk and the alpine foothills left poor Emma looking a little white, and she spent some time downstairs in their apartment before venturing further.

I was rather hoping they would enjoy a week's break on the back of a good story, so we were pleased as they filled their days with jaunts into the surrounding countryside. With one day to go before they were due to depart, however, I was beginning to think that maybe our tale wasn't worth the telling, since no interviews as such had taken place all week.

I had no cause for worry: it seemed to be simply a matter of too many options in a particularly beautiful place; they sat us down round a table groaning with wine on the eve of their departure, and we gave them our story. Also during the evening, as the cogs of communication became ever more lubricated by the continuous supply of Provençal red, we began to learn something of our interlocutors in return. Shaun, who up until this point had spoken with the diction of a professional reporter, suddenly lapsed into the broadest Norwich accent I had ever heard, and we fell about in mirth as he allowed the language of his heritage take control during the telling of some hilarious East Anglian anecdotes.

Emma spoke cautiously of babies but, as we witnessed the shocked expression on her face during the arduous evening ritual of feeding, bathing and bedding three spritely sprogs, we felt convinced that she had been put off for life.

They departed the following day with a wave and a smile, leaving us hoping against the odds that we would get at least a few lines in their newspaper to aid us with the colossal task we faced of attracting people to the gîte. A few weeks later, we received a few copies of the Eastern Daily Press through the post. We were happily impressed: I made an ugly centrefold, but the exposure was priceless.

And it seemed that the mountain air had worked another wonder: Emma announced to the world that she was expecting their first child soon afterwards.

Chapter 34

The following week we were joined by a wonderful man, whose acquaintance I had made some years earlier while on a paragliding trip to Nepal. Ian Merrylees was a thoughtful, sensitive chap, whose gentle nature was as charming as his name. When we finally met again four years after our first encounter, it was as if we had been friends for life; the intervening period had done nothing to detract from the certitude I felt that he was a truly exceptional person.

The first thing he asked me to do once settled into his weekend's accommodation was to help him learn how to fly a tandem paraglider. I had recently bought a glider capable of carrying two people; not for professional purposes, but solely for the pleasure of sharing the wonders of free flight with close friends and family, who would be able to fly with me if they were willing to accept the fact that I was no sky god, and carried no insurance into the bargain. For Ian, this didn't seem to pose a problem; the risks were reciprocated by the fact that he would be piloting the wing for the first time as a tandem pilot, and he needed me to be the guinea-pig passenger. We must have shared the same faith in each other at some level, for I felt no fear as I ran off the mountain in front of him, having previously subjected him to an extensively boring, but necessary lecture on the differences in handling characteristics between a solo and a tandem wing.

I'd been taught to fly tandem myself a few years earlier by Adam Hill, a former flying instructor from Hove in Sussex, who had subsequently embarked on an ambitious project to develop the world of free flight in Nepal. Following extensive negotiations and palm-greasing exercises with the authorities, he had managed to set up a business offering "paratreks" to those wishing to combine Himalayan trekking with flying in one of the most staggeringly beautiful corners of the planet. Adam would spend six months in the mountain kingdom, and the rest of the year back in Hove, where he was supplementing his income with a house renovation and development project.

It was during one of his stints in England – following my first, inspirational adventure with him in Nepal – that he offered to teach me how to fly a dual paraglider. As he had been a registered instructor before the Nepalese venture, we had no doubt that I would be able to receive an officially-recognised qualification on my successful completion of the tasks required for potential new pilots.

We were, however, dumbfounded to be told, after I had spent several weeks perfecting the basic skills with Adam as tutor, that since he was late in paying his annual subscription to the regulatory body concerned (he had been in Nepal for the previous six months!), his position as instructor had been nullified, and therefore his training of me would not be recognised. I asked if my training would be validated if the necessary late fee was paid, as I was trying to run a full-time business and could not envisage any free time in which to repeat the whole process for the foreseeable future. The answer was no: I would have to begin all over again with another instructor; not because I had been taught anything amiss, but simply due to the sort of British inflexibility that causes so many to seek a more humane life elsewhere.

A few rain-lashed, "unflyable" days in the Peak District in an attempt to repeat the course with another instructor was my only chance in which to become tandem-rated; thus the document proving my capabilities was not to be.

Back on the sun-soaked hills of Provence, Ian quickly adapted to the demands of the larger wing, and we spent some thrilling moments together soaring above the Col de Bleine, a site of spectacular natural splendour situated a quarter of an hour's drive west of Gréolières. Having left the ground, a pilot can rise in the warm air currents above the ridge, to be presented with a breathtaking vista of the rocky crests of the Alps to the north as the Col drops away beneath his feet. This is contrasted with the fertile greens of the valley plains on the southern side of the hill, where the landscape lies rolling and lifting towards the warm sea, finally cascading in a flurry of forested folds towards the sun-spangled beaches below.

After a few days flying me as his passenger, Ian felt confident enough to attempt a flight with a novice: someone who knew nothing about paragliding and who would therefore be a better test of his skills in handling any of the innumerable problems that can arise when flying with someone for the first time. I knew just the man.

Tony the plasterer had often asked me to take him into the sky during the final stages of the construction of the house, but, for one reason or another, we had never got round to arranging the flight.

Ian was more than happy to provide Tony with his first airborne experience, and one bright November morning the three of us headed up to the ridge above Gourdon, a decidedly quaint, medieval, tourist-tacky town. Breathtakingly built on a rocky pinnacle above the Gorges du Loup, Gourdon commands one of the best views of the Riviera coastline in the region.

I helped Ian prepare Tony for flight, and we discussed the areas in the valley where one would be most likely to find the thermals necessary for lift, so that Ian's first real tandem experience would be of reasonable duration for the pair of them. With Tony strapped in and ready to go, I rechecked the fastenings of the harnesses and the canopy itself; I had suddenly realised that, for some reason, I felt hugely responsible for their safety. I needn't have worried, as Ian's take off was exemplary and, when told to run, Tony practically tore himself out of his harness in his eagerness to get into the sky.

In fact, once off the ground, it seemed that Tony had completely forgotten to adjust his bearing as advised in order to achieve the standard, comfortable, seated position. Instead, he hung forward, suspended by the straps around the top of his legs, staring intently at the ground beneath his feet. Ian shouted down to me as they soared past on the first rising leg of their flight along the rocky ridge.

'He's hanging by his nuts! He doesn't understand my crappy French!'

I laughed at the unorthodox position Tony had adopted in his harness.

'Don't worry! He can't fall out. He'll be a bit sore though!'

Ian, reassured that all was safe up front, left the ridge and was gently lifted into the sky on the rising air, to join five or six others on their gossamer craft, like the silky seeds blown from a gigantic dandelion by some time-inquisitive giant. They gained enough height to glide out towards the village of Gourdon itself, circling above the tourists in the streets below for a time, and then rose up and back towards the cliffs and plateaus of the landscape behind the town.

They spent an hour or so in the sky, flying from ridge to ridge, from thermal to thermal, all the while poor Tony hanging limply forward in the most uncomfortable flying position I had ever seen. I made a mental note to explain the best technique of becoming seated in the harness once off the ground, then drove down to meet them at the designated landing site in the valley below.

I was met by two grinning faces as I walked into the field to collect them. Ian, hugely happy to have had a safe flight, and an extended one at that, and Tony, I presumed, excited beyond words by the pleasure that paragliding bestows upon those lucky enough to experience it.

'Well?' I enquired, as if any answer was necessary.

'You're not going to believe this!' laughed Ian.

'Believe what?' I asked.

'You know he was hanging forward in the harness, right?'

'Yeah ...'

'He was doing it on purpose! All the time I was explaining how to get back into a seated position and I thought he couldn't understand me, but he could, and he didn't care! I kept asking him if he was OK, and all the time he just stared downwards at the ground. During the flight, he kept going "Wow!" and "Whoa!" as we flew over the landscape. So I presumed he was really struck by the experience of flying. He kept pointing in different directions, so I tried to go where he wanted, and every now and then, he'd point down and go "Beautiful!", "Wow!", and stuff like that. 'Course I was pleased, I was happy that he was enjoying it so much, but when we landed, it wasn't the flying that had caused all the excitement!'

'No?' I said, 'then what was it?'

'He said ...' Ian started laughing loudly, 'he said that he'd never seen anything as beautiful as his secret cannabis empire from the air!'

I nearly died. We had witnessed the launch of a whole new paragliding application that day.

Chapter 35

The cyclic nature of the universe in which we find ourselves is, at times, irrefutably apparent in our daily lives. Things, and people, come and go; nothing lasts forever, but all is in a continual state of flux and change. To try and hold on to something material that will inevitably decay, or to attempt to hinder the eternal patterns of growth, age and death, is to fight a natural cosmic force, leading ultimately to sadness and frustration. The eastern mystics accepted this change, and the transience of existence, which in turn provided them with an inner calm and the ability to cope with life's losses in a positive and tranquil frame of mind.

During the end of December, I gained a wonderful new friend on one hand, but on the other, received the tragic news from England that one of my closest colleagues was enduring the terminal stages of cancer.

Passing the village bar one misty winter's afternoon, I noticed a character drinking within, a character I had already observed on a few occasions in and around the village. He was about sixty years of age, tall and lean, with a full head of grey, shoulder-length hair, beneath which sparkled a pair of enormous, hooped, silver earrings. He sported a hand-worked leather waistcoat of a rich red; classic cowboy boots were his choice of footwear. His rugged face wore the ecstasies and agonies of a fully indulged-in life, but his captivatingly serene blue eyes twinkled and smiled upon the world in such a peaceful, knowing manner that one felt immediately calmed in their presence. He exuded a quiet and compulsive charisma.

He was, as I had seen him before, drinking alone, and I decided to make his acquaintance if he wouldn't be offended. It transpired that he was an artist, and when I told him of my art-based English life, the foundation was provided for one of the most unique friendships I had been fortunate enough to experience.

Over several beers (the love of a good drinking session was to be another common factor in our lives), he recounted his story, although it was to be only later that I discovered the real extent of his renown: he was incredibly modest. Having been successful throughout most of his life as a professional painter, his current marriage to Björk, a striking blonde Norwegian with whom he was still very much in love, was in the process of renegotiation. As a result, he had chosen to hole up in the peace of the mountains in an attempt to regain something of his former self, and by chance in the very same village in which we had decided to escape the tedium of our own previous days. His health was also poor: he suffered from asthma and hoped that the air of the hills might ameliorate his affliction to some degree.

We became drinking partners. At eight in the evening, once the children had been bathed and bedded, I would wander into the village, or round to the rustic apartment he had temporarily rented, to share stories of life, art and music, accompanied by a few bottles, or a box, of good red wine. Karen began to joke that I now had two wives as, admittedly, the attraction of spending an evening with Eric, having spent the day in domestic bliss, began to become a frequent temptation throughout the week, although I at least endeavoured to ensure that the children were asleep before I left.

The longer I knew him, the more it seemed we had in common, and as he began to trust me, he revealed more about his exotic existence up until that point.

He had been born in the north of England and had gone to school with Dave Stewart, later to become one half of the Eurythmics, and with whom he remained good friends. He had painted since childhood and, at the age of eighteen, having deserted a formal fine art degree course, he had sold his first piece for more than his father earned in a year. At that point, he told me, his parents stopped asking him when he was going to get a "proper job".

He was one of an extremely small number of artists that I'd met who had never resorted to a conventional career to support their painting; from the age of eighteen to the present day he had been autonomous and wildly successful. As he talked to me, he cast a long arm around the room in which we sat. There was a work in progress upon the easel, and four or five others leaning against the walls, awaiting inspection by clients during the following weeks. That, he told me, was all he had of his paintings. Everything else had been sold, and always would do. I was flabbergasted.

During the seventies, he had played an instrumental part in the art movement known as "Superhumanism", made famous by the controversial gallery set up by Nicholas Treadwell, which opened in Chiltern Street, London W1, in 1968. The Chiltern Street Gallery (The Treadwell Gallery) was unique in that it concentrated on art about the basic nature of the human condition, at a time when the British art world comprised mainly hard-edged abstraction or minimalism.

Of course it was also a time of profound social change in the real world, and, in reflecting this, the gallery fast developed its controversial, even sensational, reputation. For example, during 1971, Art and Artist magazine wrote, when reviewing one of the gallery's exhibitions:

"The place blisters with works of searing eroticism, high camp, coarse belly laughs and hideous vulgarity ..."

Superhumanism itself has been defined as "art about people, people living the life of an urban society". The actual imagery of the superhumanists, while striking, and sometimes shocking, reflected the contemporary feelings of the Western experience. It was preoccupied with daily life, with the characters of the street, or characters of an obtuse nature, and with scenes depicting the emotions, stresses or potential perversions lying within each of us. The artists, while portraying their ideas in aesthetically different ways, shared a desire to convey the moving nature of their subject matter in an understandably vivid manner. A philosophic acceptance of human weakness was an important characteristic of superhumanist art, but humour, cynicism, pessimism and anger were also present, along with an almost sad observation of the human condition, emotions which were the driving forces behind some of the movement's most striking imagery.

During the years that I had been exhibiting paintings in our gallery in Norwich, I had been repelled by photographic representations of sunsets or landscape, cuddly animals or Norfolk windmills, and had refused to exhibit such paintings, even though it may have been financially beneficial. Art for me had to say something about the artist, or the world he observed, to express a feeling about a place, rather than be simply a picture of a place. For goodness' sake, if one requires a visual documentary record of a location, then the camera has admirably served the purpose for the last hundred and fifty years, or thereabouts.

So when I met Eric Scott in Gréolières and was confronted with colossal canvases painted in fine detail, I was shocked to find myself moved and awe-inspired by them. Although every minute brushstroke painstakingly reproduced its characters in staggeringly lifelike detail, this was something new. Why? Because the actual scene, the story being told, could not possibly have existed! It's one thing to copy a photograph, but totally another to paint something of which a photograph could not be taken; albeit photographically representational in style. A female body supporting the bearded head of a leering man, the artist himself being depicted surreally suspended in mid-ocean, the artist's beautiful baby boy lying cherub-like across the robed knee of his mother, masterfully depicted as the doppelganger of Christ on the knee of Mary. These scenes, or their settings, were pure fantasy, and maybe because of that, the precision of the representation imbued in their execution was powerfully emotive. I had been late to discover the art form, but felt hugely glad to have finally done so.

Also during December, it was with regret that a friend called me from Norwich to inform me that "Old John", a well-known face amongst the drinkers and philosophers of the city, had been taken seriously ill. I was distraught; John had been like a second father to me over the few years that I had had the privilege of his friendship. I booked the first flight possible back to England, leaving the ever-supportive Karen to cope with any guests alone; a job which was still being made difficult by the continual necessity to run up the road to restore the electricity supply at random intervals.

I had first met John in a run-down corner pub known as the Ironmongers, later to be converted into a faceless, frigid wine bar bearing the stomach-churningly awful moniker Boltz. At the time, however, one could wander into the comfortably scruffy back-street inn at any hour of the day, sure to be able to strike up conversation with a motley gaggle of fascinating, probably inebriated, characters from the city's bohemian street life.

One quiet afternoon, having left my sole employee, Adrian, in charge of the gallery, I drifted into the pub, and took up a position at the end of the bar from where I could best appreciate the shapely rear of the barmaid Angie. Alongside stood a quiet, short man, who appeared to be staring into the glass on the bar in front of him. After a couple of pints of delicious Adnam's bitter, my attention was diverted from Angie's incredible behind by the sound of quiet weeping. I turned to the elderly gentleman standing to my right, and saw that he was sobbing into his beer, his shaking hand barely able to support the quaking glass.

I asked him if there was anything I could do to help him: he began to calm down, and explained that he had just lost his wife after a fifty-year marriage. It transpired that she had been suffering from the horrible condition known as motor neuron disease, and he had been watching her slowly dying for the previous five years. I refreshed his pint, drew a couple of stools up to the bar, and asked him to sit down and tell me his story. I called Adrian; it looked like I was not going to be back that afternoon.

An hour or so later, I called him again and told him to close the gallery and come and join the party. John and I were already becoming pals and I was hearing things I didn't want to miss. Adrian had been a most reliable, faithful employee for many years and now and again it was good to escape the daily routine together, especially if the company was as good as John's.

He was a socialist; but not in the manner of the quasi-totalitarian governments led by recent British prime ministers, and neither following the tenets of Communism, which he described to me as "state capitalism". He urged me to read a book by William Morris, the Victorian artist, writer and social visionary.

The story he lent me the next day was entitled *News From Nowhere*, ranking among the most literary, but readable, utopian novels. The great English writer offers a compelling portrait of an ideal society in his story of a nineteenth-century man's visit to the future. William Guest (a thinly disguised Morris), falls asleep during the ugliness of the late-Victorian industrial landscape of London, waking in the twenty-second century to find England transformed into a social paradise.

In place of smog-filled streets are flowered fields of green; where quickly-built steel bridges previously existed, are now hand-crafted oak structures of incredible intricacy. Instead of financial cost being the driving force behind unattractive time-saving fabrications, all is now created with care, and for the purposes of achieving aesthetic beauty and a sense of accomplishment by the craftsman concerned. Citizens take pleasure in their work, which they regard as a form of creative expression. The whole world produces what it requires in abundance, and distributes everything according to the needs of the individual.

Morris' idyllic society reminds one of the writings of Ruskin and Marx, but forms a new and independent expression of the author's own egalitarian viewpoint. His vision of the future goes beyond previously existing systems, rejecting Communism, which had been finding favour at the time, in place of a system by which people live in harmony with the natural world. Capitalism and Communism have been eradicated, property is genuinely communal, and money therefore unnecessary. As a result, crime is virtually nonexistent, and women enjoy complete equality. *News From Nowhere* was regarded as a sentimental exercise when published in 1890. Now, with the world descending ever deeper into the filthy, bloody mire caused by the economic system in which it finds itself, I believe many will find resonance in its inspiring proposals for an alternative society.

The more John and I discussed, the more I realised why I had never been able to align myself with one or another of the political parties' ideals. It had always appeared to me that nothing really altered, once a change of government had taken place. Over the following months, as John talked of his politically active life and beliefs, I was gradually coming to the conclusion that all my own theories for the future sanity of the planet could also be realised if the one common factor we believed in was to ever come about – a world without money.

It is all blindingly obvious once one considers the huge ramifications of a change such as this. It has constantly depressed me to see bread mountains growing in Europe on the one hand, while thousands of African children starve to death on the other. To witness massive quantities of grain being burnt so as to maintain its market price here, while millions of undernourished babies die there. What madness is this?

The capitalist system demands profit, and therefore there will always be losers. And on the lowest rungs of this inhuman ladder are the poorest wage slaves, earning pennies, while the products they create are sold to brainwashed westerners at ludicrously inflated prices.

It is widely accepted that six million Jews (as well as millions of other, and, for some reason, less-publicised victims) were killed by Hitler during the Second World War. It is now estimated that *sixty* million civilians have been annihilated in twenty-nine separate invasions by America of other states since the end of that war, campaigns to assert western economic dominance by aggressively attempted takeover of the planet's money-making resources, no matter where they be.

With our modern communications systems, the citizens of the planet could be integrated as a workforce, each one giving according to his ability. Jobs required to produce things could be rotated to eliminate boredom, along with the revolting condition in which human beings are chained daily to the inhuman screens in front of them, dying slowly for years on end. A myriad of skills and talents are being suffocated by the set-up in which we find ourselves, a structure in which it is normal to suffer from depression and fatigue, largely brought about by the unnatural, artificial working environments demanded of us by the economic system in which we are expected to function.

We implore our children to share their toys, or their sweets, because we know instinctively that the human being is a social species, depending on positive, peaceful relationships with others to achieve happiness. At what point in a child's life does the sharing stop? And why? Because capitalism demands, contrary to natural human instincts, that we guard our own, and keep the poor in poverty. In the timeless words of Pink Floyd:

> "Money, get back.
> I'm alright Jack keep your hands off of my stack.
> Money, it's a hit.
> Don't give me that do goody good bullshit."

Yes, indeed, after teaching our children to do good to others, the financial system's propaganda machine necessarily destroys within its teenage citizens all such human kindness, since it would collapse if we were not brainwashed into accepting mean, egotistical ideals and the desire to possess.

To an alien being observing the Earth from afar, it would be laughable that now, in the twenty-first century, we are still blowing each other to bits in order to control parts of the tiny planet that we've overrun. Why on earth, with all our technology, are we still dropping bombs on each other on a daily basis? It's not even as if we've got anywhere else to go when we've completely fucked it all up.

My friend John had attended many demonstrations during his life, but had come to the conclusion, as I was beginning to realise myself, that reformism is a futile quest. Politicians have a price. Their decisions are a direct result of the "Fat Cats'" financial input into their party or private lives.

The American president, for example, is necessarily a non-thinking nonentity; an easily-manipulated glove-puppet on the hands of the billionaire oil barons and weapons manufacturers in his cabinet. The English prime minister is his poodle; either threatened or paid to indulge the vacuous president on his killing sprees. Until the system that depends upon money is superseded by something more in keeping with the potential creativity and artistic aspirations of the human mind, no protests, marches or demonstrations are going to make an iota of a scintilla of a difference.

It appears that there is no true democracy in the West. The decisions are made by, and in the interests of, commerce, while the people are cleverly placated by the illusionary belief that they have a say, or a vote. The whole political charade is played out daily in the news, diverting attention from what is really being done by the instigators of policy as they fill their pockets with the blood-stained spoils of their despicable crusades.

A non-violent world may seem like a utopian dream. And you may call me a dreamer. But I know I'm not the only one. And if we don't dream and strive for something better, then how will the world ever change at all? Imagine (and why not, for God's sake?) "all the people sharing all the world". The elimination of the man who penned those words, the true import of which are so threatening to the materialistic American Dream (Nightmare!), is perhaps not such a mystery after all.

Our shared desire to see a world in which people could live in peace was not the only thing I had in common with my fascinating new friend. We shared a tendency to drink a lot of real ale; after three or four pints, I would ask my ruddy-faced companion if he'd like another one:

'What?!' he'd retort, 'I'm jusht getting the tashte for it ...'

John loved music, and a catholic selection to boot. On the few occasions I managed to visit his Victorian terraced house, we listened to Mozart followed by Freddy Mercury at ear-splitting volume. We both had a fondness for roots reggae, but I was now introduced to the original Rude Boy sound of the Jamaican fifties, and was fascinated when John produced an authentic Prince Buster album from 1961 for my delectation. He also delighted in art, and had created many expressively colourful pieces which adorned the walls of his bohemian home. He grew organic cannabis of the highest quality, and brewed fruit wines, which he referred to as "rocket fuel".

Over the three years I knew him before we left for our new home in France, he would pop into Frames of Norwich on a regular basis, giving me the perfect excuse to accompany him to the nearest hostelry at times when he missed his dear wife or simply needed some company. I recall several occasions when Adrian, seeing John shuffling into the shop, would turn to me sighing, and say:

'Oh, well, Ben, see you tomorrow ...'

His long face would be transformed into an excited grin as I guiltily invited him to join us.

The first time that I visited John after hearing of his illness, I was shocked to see the stocky frame of my friend reduced to a frail spectre of his former self. By the third time I managed to get back to England, in late January, he had become so unrecognisable that I had to choke back the tears as he opened his front door to me. He was bent double, his watery eyes staring up out of huge, grey, hollow sockets. The man of seventy-two appeared thirty years older, wasted by the sickening ravages of cancer.

I had brought Francesca and Emily to say "Hello" to him, as they remembered him from opening evenings at the gallery, but it was really, I knew as soon as I set eyes on the poor man, "Goodbye". They were visibly troubled by his appearance, so, having given him some drawings they had made for him during the flight back to England, I dropped them off at the Norwich home of Esther, my sister, promising to return soon. I went back with a bottle of wine, and sat with my arm around his withered shoulders as we tried to thwart the present by recounting stories from the past.

He had boldly made a hopeless promise to me on the previous visit I had made, to the effect that, as soon as he was better, he would be over to see us in our new house. I promised him that I would return to escort him, as I had done with my own dear father, and said we would drink wine on the terrace together in the warm sunshine.

Now, however, such courageous pretence was futile. As I sat on the arm of his chair, his head pressed closely against my troubled heart, he asked one thing of me.

'Ben?' he asked, quietly. 'Is there a mountain near your house?'

'Yes, John,' I replied shakily, 'the house is built on the side of a beautiful mountain.' It was becoming difficult to talk.

'Ben, promise me this: when you walk on the mountain, find somewhere you think I would have liked. Make a small cairn by the side of the path. Every time you pass, remember me and place a rock there for me. That's all.'

I could only nod firmly in promise as my tears fell heavily into his thinning hair.

Chapter 36

John's funeral was held in a Norwich crematorium and, in keeping with his beliefs, the ceremony was conducted by one of his humanist friends. The congregation listened to a précis of his life, interspersed by musical interludes of classical and reggae recordings. The small chapel was packed with a crowd of mourners of all ages and social status; a mark of the unique affability and popularity of the chap among young and old alike.

My son Jo returned from university in London expressly for the occasion. He, as I, had loved the old man like a second father, and had spent many an hour with him alone, or accompanied by friends, the attraction of John's remarkably refreshing philosophies and a smoke of his finest home-grown produce obliterating the generation gap between them.

We celebrated John's life back at the terraced house in which he had lived for many years. Everything was still as it had always been, accentuating the glaring absence of our friend. His daughter Rachel was generous enough to let me select my favourite paintings from John's collection, pictures which graphically portrayed, in their colourful and abstract expressionism, a soul of quiet strength and profound intoxication with the vibrancy of life.

The third death of someone with whom I had shared a powerful paternal or fraternal bond threw into sharp perspective any of the other daily difficulties and challenges which we had been experiencing around that time.

I returned from John's funeral imbued with a bizarre sense of extreme loss associated with a very real optimism. Ian, Dad and now John had unexpectedly passed away in the space of a year and a half, each one of them having relished the idea of sharing some special times with us once the house had been completed. Sadly, not one of them was to see the final realisation of our hopes and dreams, but the truncation of their lives served only to reinforce my long-held conviction that we had done the right thing. From now on, I told myself, I would endeavour to see each new day as a gift – a bonus provision from the great warehouse of existence – and to derive, wherever possible, the maximum pleasure from our magnificent new environment and the daily joy provided by the smiles upon the faces of our children.

During late February we finally received a phone call from the proprietor of the neighbouring parcel of land. She had called us in response to countless requests for her permission to erect the pole we needed to end the seemingly interminable wait for a proper electricity supply to the house and the inevitable, frequent blackouts.

'Hallo? Monsieur Moss?'

'Yes, speaking.'

'Hallo. Apparently, you want permission for some sort of electrical installation on my land? I've been away, I'm afraid, and have only just been made aware of your demands.'

A wild tsunami of relief submerged me in a blissful turquoise world of bubbles and light. At last!

'Yes, that's right.' She must have been able to hear the way my words smiled happily down the line to her. 'Our new home has been built for some time now, and we can't get the proper electricity supply to the house until you give the "OK" for the cable to be brought along the perimeter of your terrain, by the roadside.'

'Hmm, I'm not sure about that.'

Wrong answer.

'B ... but, Madame, it simply involves another wooden post right beside the road; just like the one that's already there! It won't be actually obstructing anything on your land in the least.'

My voice, joyfully expectant just a few moments before, was becoming a strangled whine as I desperately implored her to see common sense.

'Well, that's for me to decide. You'll have to give me some time.'

I was aghast. I simply could not cope with this new twist. After months of running a hundred metres up the road every time the meter tripped due to us having any more than the absolute minimum of clients resident below, my patience was wearing thinner than a dieting Kate Moss on a coke binge.

'Alright,' I spat through grindingly clenched teeth, 'let us know as soon as you've reached a decision. Oh, and meanwhile, it may interest you to know that, until we get a proper power supply sorted out, my children are being deprived of heating in their bedrooms.'

Not entirely true, but it was certainly the case that all electrical appliances in the house would have to be switched off when the meter tripped, in order to safeguard the supply to our guests; although thankfully, at the time, business was still extremely patchy.

Exercising her rights to the letter, we were made to wait during three further weeks of suspense while the lady made up her mind. And what we had heard appeared to be the case: she not only lived an hour's drive from the small, non-constructible piece of land in question, she had never been seen by anyone in the village, and apparently spent much of the year in America. Perhaps some of that country's Puritan inflexibility was rubbing off on her.

However, using the electricity company as mediator, she finally acquiesced. Ultimately sensing the conclusion of a particularly tedious sub-chapter in the story of our lives, I excitedly called the electricity board to arrange the final installation and thus the eventual increase in amperage to the house, bringing an end to the frantic chases along a dark lane at ridiculous hours of the night.

'I'm sorry, Monsieur, installation of your definitive power supply is impossible at present.'

Oh, no. Not again. My high spirits went into freefall; my inflated optimism shrank like a scrotum in a Siberian sea. What on God's good Earth could possibly be the matter now?

'But surely,' I limply replied, 'everything is in place that's required?'

'No, Monsieur. We have still not received the Certificate of Conformity for the interior work. When was the installation inside the house completed?'

By now, I was beyond all rational levels of thought and control.

'Fucking ages ago!' I screamed into the phone. (It was actually the French equivalent, but bear with me here; nothing quite portrays my tone at the time as well as the use of the obvious English expletive.)

'Well, sir, then I suggest you talk to your electrician, who should have arranged for an inspection of the installation on completion of his work. We can't do anything until we've received the required certificate confirming that all's been done correctly.'

Of course. As in England. And, as in England, if one pays an electrician in the order of a thousand pounds a week one would expect that he would know what he was doing. On top of that, Peter had told us that this was the cash price to avoid the twenty per cent TVA (VAT) charges! In all due respect, his standard of work was impeccable. But since, as we later found out, he had never wired a new house from scratch before (being more used to refurbishments of existing establishments) he had never actually encountered the need to submit an application for the Certificate of Conformity for a new residence.

Simmering with disbelief at this further complication, I called Peter as soon as I had finished with the electricity company, and he agreed to fill in the required forms on our behalf. He would then submit them to the authority responsible for checking standards in the field as soon as he could manage it; although, since he was in the middle of a huge electrical installation for the forthcoming Cannes Film Festival, it would take him a week or three. Oh, and we had better prepare ourselves for the rather high level of fees involved with such an inspection.

We drank a lot of wine that evening.

Chapter 37

March saw the second club booking by our friend Andrew of Flying Frenzy, the paragliding school from Dorset. With just two weeks to go before his arrival, we were at last visited by the chap who would be able to issue us with the means to increase our power supply.

Andrew's pilots had been hugely long-suffering during the incessant blackouts which had occurred with frightening regularity throughout their previous stay in the autumn: we had assured them the problem would be resolved before they returned.

As the electrical inspector prodded and poked his way around the delightfully neat wiring system in the house, I could almost feel the Certificate of Conformity in my grasp, like a priceless "Golden Ticket" in the hands of a small chocolate-lover. In our case, however, we were to receive a lifetime's supply of sweetly sufficient levels of power.

All went well until the man descended the railway-sleeper steps towards the holiday apartments on the lower level of the house. He wandered in and around the three lodgings, then, emerging from the third, scratched his head and squinted up at me, a pensive look upon his face.

'Excuse me, Monsieur, but these apartments don't seem to be connected.'

'Well, no,' I replied, 'they're independent lettings for holidaymakers and the like.'

'So they all have individual entrances, and are unreachable from inside your house?' He was catching on fast.

'Exactly. A person renting an apartment would hardly wish to be awakened by a small child leaping on his head at five in the morning demanding an early rendering of *The Three Billy Goats Gruff* now, would he?' My facetious tone belied a creeping sensation from which I knew for a certain that something horrible was about to happen.

'Well, monsieur, I'm afraid that this building constitutes four individual dwellings: your house, plus three apartments. As they are not internally connected that means you must submit four applications for inspections for electrical conformity, not just one as you have done. And then we will return to examine the four installations.'

Goggle-eyed, bottom jaw hanging somewhere around my knees, head uncontrollably bobbing about like one of those plastic dogs which used to adorn the parcel shelves of cars owned by a strange type of motorist, it was all I could do to stop myself sinking to my knees and sobbing wretchedly into my palms. He shook my quivering hand and took leave of us, just pausing to mention that the three apartments also needed individual fuse boards; not a collective one as Peter had installed for them.

There are times in one's life during which, unless one makes a superlative effort to see the bigger picture and appreciate the truly important stuff, one runs a serious risk of mental breakdown, beaten into a psychological pulp by the inanity of the system in which we function. I recalled my personal pledge made following John's funeral, and made an earnest effort to get things into perspective. We had our health, the sun was shining, and our growing circle of friends comprised some of the loveliest people we had had the good fortune to meet.

We filled in three more forms, paid the inspection fee in quadruplicate, employed Peter to assist me in installing three complete new fuse boards for the apartments, and awaited the second visit from the doom-laden inspector. He called Peter on receipt of the forms.

'Thank you for the extra forms and fees, monsieur. Have you installed the additional fuse boards as recommended?'

'Yes,' replied Peter.

'Oh, well, it's a long way to come again. I'll take your word for it. The certificates will be in the post.'

And that, astonishingly enough, was that. Four fees. Four applications. Three thousand euros' worth of extra wiring, trunking, switches and fuse boards. And no second inspection.

I often wonder: why?

It sometimes seems that some things exist purely to frustrate us. To confuse and confound us. To muddle and mystify us. To bemuse, baffle and bewilder us. For which there are no answers. For which it's best to simply not ask the questions, as in: The Meaning of Life, The Existence of God, Life After Death, The Topless Dustpan, and, of course, The Disintegrating CD Case.

When I was a lot younger, having swept the debris of a given area into a small pile, it was not a complicated matter to transport such waste with the aid of a simple device known as a dustpan and brush.

One brushed the dust into the pan – a straightforward receptacle which resembled a large mouth with a handle – enabling one to deposit the sweepings into a bin nearby.

There came a period, however, when the people who made the "pan" part of the ensemble decided to give Mr. Logic a particularly long holiday, during which time they employed a part-time lunatic in his place. A madman, who decided that it might be better to leave the upper part of the pan off, to produce a pan without a roof or cover, a pan which would make the simple act of collecting dust become a nightmarish task of Herculean proportions. Why, now one could watch the dust as it was swept towards the pan, to continue up and over the back and sides in a great grimy fountain of powdery dirt, to fall in a random formation across the floor, providing the exciting and repeated opportunity of restarting the whole cleaning process.

A remarkably progressive step in domestic technology indeed, matched only by the breathtakingly deficient design of the plastic case housing the contemporary compact disc. In no other field can I conceive of an item intended for regular opening and closing whose hinge points spontaneously disintegrate at any given time during the first few days of their usage. Of course, at the laboratory stage, such ideas are tested and rejected at regular intervals, in order to arrive at a design suitably robust for their intended application.

So what the blazes was going on at CD Case Inc. when what passes for an appropriate container for the modern CD was staggeringly released into the marketplace ... ?

'Ere, Bill, nice bit 'o weed this, mate ...'

'Yeah, cool, Terry ... aaah ... right, yeah, cool.'

''Ey, Bill ... hee, hee ... see that final working prototype for the CD case ... oooh ... aaah ... mmm ... hee, hee ... y'know, the one that won't fall apart even after it's been opened and closed ten thousand times ... ?'

'Wha–? Yeah...hee, hee...wotovit?'

'Heh, hehehe, what 'say we swop it fer this plastic toy one? Hee, hee ... 'magine the boss's face when 'e presents it to the Board on Friday an' it falls apart in 'is 'ands! Heh, heh ...'

'Hehehe, yeah, man, what like they wouldn't notice it ... come on, man ...'

Yeah, right, only no one did notice it. And they haven't noticed it for nigh on twenty years.

There are no answers. Best to just not ask the questions. And so it was with our electricity supply. All questions evaporated into thin air as we were finally given a date for the installation of the new meter outside our house, allowing for the increase in amperage we so desperately needed in order to obviate the midnight marathons to which we had become so reluctantly accustomed.

An amusing anecdote to the episode was the fact that I had misinterpreted a particularly technical part of the original documentation: there was no post actually required to be installed on our neighbour's land after all; the simple need being merely a reinforcing cable from an existing pole into a rock situated on the very edge of the highway. A rock, whose other side projected just thirty centimetres into the land forming the property of our neighbour.

Chapter 38

My friendship with Eric Scott had been deepening during the early days of the year. We spent many hours together, usually accompanied by copious quantities of good red, and it was with surprise and delight that I listened to the stories of his life up to that point. He had been commissioned to paint portraits by people from all walks of life, but being not only modest, and sometimes decidedly dismissive of the phenomenon known as "celebrity", it took a while before I unearthed some of the more legendary names amongst his client list.

Eric had painted portraits for Paul McCartney, Mick Jagger and Jerry Hall (with whom he remained firm friends), Marvin Gaye, Joni Mitchell, Andy Mackay (of Roxy Music), Phil Palmer and Mark Knopfler (of Dire Straits), Frankie Vaughan, Brian Ferry and Sting, and of course his old chums Dave Stewart and Annie Lennox. In fact, it had been Eric's joint portrait of the Eurythmics which adorned the cover of their highly-acclaimed album *Revenge.*

He had lived on the West Coast of America for a while and, due to his reputation in the music industry, went on to receive commissions from the lights of the film world. Anthony Quinn, Derek Jacobi, Jimmy Nail and film director Ridley Scott, along with his brother Tony, had all had their portraits painted by Eric. Even such diverse names as Glenda Jackson MP, Harold Wilson MP, Prince Murat, and George Barrie (of Fabergé) were to be found among Eric's list of clients for portraiture. About a year or so before I met Eric, Robbie Williams had also succumbed to the magic of Mr Scott. While visiting the gallery that Eric had previously owned with Björk at Les Adrets, inland from St Tropez, he had bought thirteen of Eric's pieces in an enthusiastic display of sincere appreciation of the artist's unique ability.

One evening, having recounted the story of his love affair with the girl whom Brian Jones had been courting at the time of his mysterious death in a friend's swimming pool, Eric asked if I had any ideas as to how he might re-establish himself on the British scene, having spent many years in other climes. His agent Arna, the wife of my friend Bruce Goldsmith of Gréolières, had been promoting his work in the region, but they were now in Brazil for several weeks, where Bruce was competing as part of the British team for the World Paragliding Championship. I detected a sense of urgency in Eric's voice.

'It's not as if I've got fuckin' forever, Ben,' he said to me. 'Here I am, still madly in fuckin' love with Björk but we can't fuckin' live together, holed up in a beautiful place but feeling fuckin' cut off, an' I want to get back in the fuckin' big time. Arna's working here for me, but hey, can you think of anything we could do to set England alight? I'm getting fuckin' bored.' (His calm way of speaking and his soft, vocal tone somehow tempered the effect of the ubiquitous expletive which littered his conversations.)

I assured him that I would try to think of some way in which my former art-world connections could be used to his advantage, while respecting the fact that he already had an agent in France. I certainly did not wish to tread on the toes of my friends in that regard. We threw some ideas around the table and, over the ensuing few days, began to form the embryo of an idea for a possible exhibition project, one discussion taking place in the attractive bar situated in the square at Cipières.

It was mid-way through the evening, as I ordered our third pints, that Sabine, the proprietor, surprised me when she tentatively said:

'Er, I'm really not sure if I can give you any more, Ben.'

This was strange. In the words of Old John, I was just getting the taste for it, and certainly was not, at that point, at all drunk.

'Sorry, Sabine, I don't understand,' I replied, 'don't I appear sober?'

'Oh, no!' she laughed, 'it's not that, Ben! It's simply that I would rather you settle up with what you owe us from before. We don't mind giving credit to you, of course, but it has been a while now.'

I could not think for the life of me what she was referring to.

'But, Sabine,' I continued, 'I haven't been in here for months!'

'Exactly, Ben! Remember the night when you were in here until about three in the morning with Bob?'

I did. My friend Bob the paraglider pilot, myself and others had indeed spent a very jolly time in the bar at one point, leaving happily oblivious at some ridiculous hour of the night. But that had been over a year ago!

'What?!' I gasped, as I began to understand the predicament in which I now found myself. 'You mean I didn't settle up on the night, Sabine?'

'No, Ben. You drank far more than you could pay for, but assured me that you'd sort it out the next day. We really ought to get it settled, eh?' She was now smiling, and Eric laughed loudly.

I felt small as I was impressed by yet another incident revealing the hugely laid-back attitude of our French friends of the region. I had remembered not much at all the next day, and now a whole year had passed before they politely wished to remind me of my dues! And they were considerable. As Eric and I pulled thirstily on the foaming beer now being granted us, I assured the ever-patient Sabine that I would endeavour not to let such an oversight occur again.

One March morning, as the soft spring sunshine poured like honey over the languid landscape, Eric invited me to accompany him to his favourite art supplies shop in Cannes. During the trip, he hoped we'd be able to crystallise our plan for an attention-grabbing show in England, and also pass an hour or two supping beers on the boulevard which faced the harbour.

It was to be a day of momentous catharsis, and one which will remain etched upon my memory for the rest of my life.

Having crammed Eric's red Mercedes to the roof with canvas, paints and a diverse selection of brushes, we retired to a pavement table at a café in the festival-goers' district known as La Croisette, and sat for a while admiring the beauty, or despising the pretence, of those that passed us by. As the waiter arrived with our drinks, Eric hit upon a staggeringly simple, yet uniquely impressive idea for an exhibition of maximum impact.

'Y'know, Ben?' he said. 'What about a one-picture show? I mean a fuck-off massive painting that no one could miss?'

'Hmm?' I replied. 'What? Just one painting in the exhibition?'

'Yep. One fucking huge painting that we tour round the world. Gotta get noticed. What d'you think?'

I thought. I drank. I thought some more. Maybe it was the sun, the beer and the ambience of the Riviera in springtime, but the more I thought, the more I realised that Eric had spawned an inspirationally incredible idea. A huge canvas painted in superhumanist style. Undiluted by others being exhibited in its presence. A painting that the whole world would come to recognise. A painting that everyone would want to see. And, even if it were sold, a painting which would continue to be toured until Eric was once again a household name across the world. The nature of the exhibition would, in itself, attract attention, let alone the painter himself. As far as I knew, it was a totally novel conception. It was a brilliant stroke of genius by the man, it filled me with an electrifying enthusiasm, and I knew at that moment that it was going to work. We were about to embark on a special adventure together.

As we smilingly sipped at our beers, there remained only to find the subject matter worthy of such large-scale execution and notoriety.

It was whilst we were turning our attention to this conundrum that I, for some reason or other, thought once more of my father, and how excited he would have been at a moment like this. I must have verbalised my musings.

'Did you say your father died fairly recently?' Eric asked me.

'Yeah, strangely enough while he was actually on his way out here to see me.'

'Fuck. Really?'

'Mmm, it was awful. There I was, working on the house, just about to leave for Nice to pick him and my brother up, when I got a call to say he'd collapsed and died on the way. In the rush hour in a London station.'

'Oh, no! That's bad. When was this?'

'January last year. The twenty-second. The day before my fortieth birthday.'

'January. End of January. That's fuckin' weird ...'

'Weird? Why?'

'Twenty-second. Yeah ... King's Cross ...'

I choked on my beer and sat bolt upright.

'How the fuck did you know that?!' I blurted.

'Listen,' Eric replied, 'tell me more. Was it in the morning? About nine-thirty or thereabouts?'

I was overwhelmed with a sense of expectation, almost hopefulness, but also the terror that a virtually tenable piece of information of mind-blowing importance might somehow yet slip from my grasp. As if ... if I proceeded further with this fantastically bizarre inquiry, it may somehow fail to bear some fruit for which I so desperately longed, but couldn't bring myself to accept may be credible. My emotional optimism got the better of me, however, and I begged Eric to continue.

'This is so fucking weird, Ben. My son Beau; you've met him once I think? He's in his late teens; was here last year, remember? We were sitting outside Claudine's bar in the village and I introduced you. I hardly knew you myself then, of course.'

There was no way I could have forgotten the striking beauty of Eric's son, and his mild manner, so like that of his father.

'Go on,' I said, in nervous anticipation.

'Beau had also been to visit me on an earlier occasion, that same week your dad died. When he arrived, he seemed upset. He told me he'd witnessed an elderly man collapsing near some stairs at King's Cross Station, and the experience had really unsettled him. It was the morning of January the 22nd, Ben!'

I sat, frozen, my head in turmoil, as the full impact of what I was hearing began to become clear to me.

What were the chances of an artist of Eric's status choosing exactly the same village as ourselves in which to escape the pressures of the limelight for a while? And what were the chances of his son travelling to visit him on exactly the same day that my father had chosen to visit us? Then, what chance of passing through the same station, in the same city, even though his journey originated in a completely different part of the country from that of my dad's? And at exactly the same time, on the very same stairway, among thousands of other people, to witness my dear father's collapse and death!

The saddest aspect of my father's passing had been that no one was there. He had had no family around him; he had died anonymously in the rush hour in a crowded station stairwell, leaving a vast empty space in my consciousness in which, it had seemed, unanswered questions would never find their resolution.

But I now had a direct connection to someone who had been there at that very moment; someone who I knew could now help me unravel the mystery surrounding the actual circumstances of the event, and thus finally help me lay to rest some deeply-felt uncertainties: it was to be a profoundly moving experience meeting Eric's son again some months later. But for now, as the gloriously luminous light of the Côte d'Azur shattered into a million pieces upon the dancing waves before me, I felt, almost tangibly, the beginning of a healing process somewhere within my being, and the calming knowledge that now, at last, I could begin to live for the future in peace once again.

Chapter 39

The extraordinary sequence of coincidences that now connected us led to a deepening of our mutual friendship, and Eric would hug me like a son when we came across each other in the village or at our homes. Each evening, he was in the habit of taking an aperitif in the village bar, following which he would amble across the small square to the welcoming warmth of La Pierre à Feu, to be greeted enthusiastically by Thierry and Lyn, who would show him to the fireside table at which he would always sit.

I was not in a position to dine out every evening, but would join Eric for a carafe of wine as often as family commitments would allow. Over the ensuing weeks, we drew together the threads that would result in one of the most remarkable contemporary exhibitions to be seen for many years. It was during one such soirée in the cosy restaurant – having swapped anecdotes, memories and special moments from exhibitions, private views and the art of life in general – when talk of pictures, portraits and personalities led us to the solution of the subject matter for the enormous canvas Eric was about to create. He had been considering a landscape, but I dissented.

'Surely you've become known as a portraitist? What about a mammoth portrait of someone instantly recognisable?' I suggested.

'Mmm, but who? Who would want a portrait unless it was theirs?' Eric countered.

'I'm not so sure. Faces of unique and well-known individuals can be popular. I mean, is there a special anniversary or celebration in the air? There's always the Queen,' I said wryly, ribbing the man.

'Fuck off! I only paint real fucking people, Ben. Not fuckin' cardboard cut-outs.'

I laughed. 'Yeah, I know. What about a rock star that you know, that everyone loves?'

'Now you're fuckin' talking! Hmm ...'

I tried to think of all the people of whom Eric had spoken, those whom he had loved, those whom he had hated for their pretence, and those whom he still respected enough to commit to a project of such gargantuan proportions. It was obvious.

'The Stones! The fucking Stones!' I was at it now.

'He ... e ... y! Yes! Mick and Keith, maybe the others ... That's it! That's it!'

I was pleased that the suggestion had gone down well, but I wasn't quite sure how it could be done.

'Ben! I've just finished a portrait for Keith Richards! It's nearly two metres tall by about a metre and a half broad. I'll do the others in the same style, you make a fuck-off great frame for the four portraits and there's the exhibition! I'll paint it, you organise the fucker!'

'Unbelievable!' I was flying now.

Back in England, it had sometimes been so hard to get any sort of media coverage for art shows, even if the body of work we were exhibiting was of an extremely high standard. I would spend hours on the phone to newspapers, local radio and television stations in rarely successful attempts to get some promising new talent any form of exposure or acknowledgement for their artistic abilities. But to publicise this, with Eric's notoriety and legendary list of clients, was going to be child's play. Having left the commercial art world in the wake of emigration, or so I had thought, I was now being asked to set up an exhibition for which the marketing would be easier than anything with which I had previously been confronted. A gift, on a plate. Boxed, wrapped and ribboned.

It was of little interest to either of us whether the picture itself sold; Eric desperately wanted to be appreciated again: we were going to sell the artist. We were going to put the master back in the limelight, for his own sense of worth and for the benefit of his audience. This was going to be pure theatre, and we both knew it. We were going to have a party.

Chameleon season. Alpine snowlines. Sun-happy valley. April proclaimed change, rode the tumescent tide of growth and surging life, and finally crashed, satisfied and spent, upon the soothing shores of summer's dawn. The spring rains spelt sparse business for the gîte, but allowed me the time I needed to organise Eric's English revival, whilst Icelandic Arna continued to build the man's notoriety on her home ground – the French Riviera and Scandinavia.

I sat in our small upstairs office, phone in hand, and began to piece together the campaign that would regain the artist the recognition he deserved back in England. This wasn't the selling of a product, but a personality. It was the delightful task of bringing people together, the audience and the creator, of exhibiting one of the most impressive paintings I had ever seen to the maximum number of admirers, and I relished the task.

Although having been born in Bromley, Kent, most of my adult life had been spent in the provincial purlieus of Norwich, the East Anglian capital, and it was here that I would initially be able to expose Eric's work with the least difficulty. Norwich: once second in importance only to London in the country, and still forming the most complete medieval city remaining in England.

Firstly, the venue. I recalled the Forum, a gargantuan, glassy structure in the city centre – the winner of a national award for contemporary architecture – housing the new library and a vast exhibition space, usually shared by three or four independent hirers. It would be ideal, but must be given over to the one show. I called the City Hall and finally made contact with a lady responsible for the space, who at first seemed reluctant to rent the whole area to a sole artist.

'Erm, we haven't done that before, Mr Moss. We're normally familiar with our exhibitors, so would have to be sure of the quality of the work. Maybe you should send us some examples of his painting ability before we can discuss this matter further.'

She obviously imagined watercolours of country villages, or miniature oils of cats, flowers or a bunch of grapes. Once I had explained who the artist actually was, and that she could see a very good example of his work on album sleeves in any high-street record shop, her reticence gave way to enthusiasm, and she promised me she would do all she could to help promote the show. We pencilled in some dates for the end of July – the timescale Eric had indicated would be necessary to complete the remaining three Rolling Stones portraits – and I moved on to the media.

A journalist at the *Eastern Daily Press*, one of England's biggest provincial rags at the time, was eager to meet Eric ahead of the exhibition, and suggested we fly out forthwith for an in-depth interview, when we could also tie up with reporters from local television and radio (Anglia Television and BBC East were equally excited by the project). The final job was to arrange the flights, which Eric booked for Saturday the seventh of May; interviews and meetings with sponsors were scheduled to be held on the Monday and Tuesday thereafter.

We devised a scaffolding system to suspend the huge canvas above the floor in the centre of the exhibition space, and Karen occupied herself over the next few days with calling various contractors who would be able to meet Eric and me during the promotional trip to Norwich to help us finalise the design. It was all becoming rather fun; especially when I discovered that the opening night of the show would coincide with Mick Jagger's birthday; and the year also saw the fortieth anniversary of the release of *Satisfaction.*

With all parties in England primed for our visit in the early part of May, I dropped in to Eric's place one evening to discuss the frame he would require for the picture, smugly thinking I had done quite well up to that point. I explained everything that I had arranged – including the supply, from various second-hand dealers in the city of Norwich, of several copies of the Revenge album cover with which to dress the exhibition – then felt small as he asked the obvious question.

'Great, man, but where do we go from Norwich?'

I had no answer to that one, although, given our contacts, I truly believed that the stir created by the exhibition would facilitate the easy location of a space in London or elsewhere, since we had decided to continue to tour the picture even if someone actually wanted to buy it en route. There was no need for concern, however.

Eric had been busy.

'Hey, Ben, don't worry. It's lookin' good, man! I've got Dave Stewart checking out a venue in LA, and my friend Matthew, the New Yorker, is getting somewhere sorted out in the fuckin' Big Apple!

'And, you know Arna's got some shows arranged in Scandinavia for my other stuff? One of those guys wants me to ask Annie Lennox to open the show. I'm gonna tell them to fuck off and ask her agent – I hate it when they try to use me like that, the bastards – but anyway, we'll take the Stones up there, too, eh?'

We celebrated with a box of wine, and I meandered home contentedly through the warmth of the night.

A few days before our reconnaissance trip to England, Eric and I travelled down to a woodyard near the coast to select some material with which to construct the colossal frame. The finished structure was to be collapsible, in order to facilitate easy transportation of all the various components comprising the exhibition. We were also planning to fabricate a large box in which the four portraits and the frame components could be packed and shipped to wherever the next venue proved to be.

The woodyard was situated in the charming medieval village of Biot, just minutes from the coast which, by chance, Eric told me, had been the location of his first Riviera residence on his return from Los Angeles. The place was staffed by an amicable chap, who immediately understood what we required and led us over to a large pile of well-seasoned, flat, pine planking. Since Eric intended to decorate the surface of the frame himself, we selected some suitable lengths of broad profile and, business being done for the day, retired to the village centre for a beer under the welcome shade of the trees adorning the square.

It was here that Eric told me more about the pretty girl he had met at a camping site years earlier; a girl with whom he had fallen in love long before he discovered that her previous lover had been Brian Jones of the Rolling Stones, the demise of whom is still shrouded in mystery to this very day.

Maybe it was the heat of the afternoon, or the beers we had enjoyed together, but I detected, or so it seemed to me, a distinct breathlessness about the man that afternoon as we ascended the short slope to the car park ahead of our journey back into the hills behind the coast.

The next day, laying the wood out on the terrace behind our house, the only flat surface on our property large enough to cope with the size of the intended construction, we discussed the various logistical options for the fabrication of the biggest picture frame I had ever been asked to produce. In keeping with its proportions, we decided to assemble all of its ten joints using a system of huge chrome bolts, lending a heavy industrial appearance to the whole affair. There would be vertical dividing struts separating each portrait, with broader planks being used for the surrounding sides. The four paintings would therefore be individually framed but, at the same time, form composite members of an almighty whole, like small panes in a larger window design. The final, overall dimensions were a little daunting: over six metres in length by two and a half metres deep.

'It's enormous!' I exclaimed, once having seen the contrivance sprawled out across the terrace.

'Yep!' Eric concurred, 'an' it's your job to put it together! See you in the bar at six? Have a good 'un!'

I was left staring down at the thing, scratching my head.

Chapter 40

Friday the sixth of May. The village bar, 8.30 a.m. A bright, springy morning of butterflies and birdsong. As I sauntered back from escorting Emily to school, I noticed that Claudine's small bar-room was more than usually busy for the day, so decided to take a coffee and join the jolly banter within.

Eric sat at his usual place at the end of the room, facing the bar, the world and its occupants being casually observed through the brilliant blue eyes of the artist. He was, as ever, colourfully but elegantly garbed, today in a shirt of riotous red, and was grinning contentedly.

'Hey, Ben! Beautiful day! Have a coffee?'

'Yeah, sure!' I happily replied, always pleased to spend time in the man's company.

We were both eagerly looking forward to the next day's trip to England and the subsequent preparations for the big show; the buoyant mood we shared seemed to be almost tangible in the atmosphere.

'So, how's it going, mate?' I asked Eric, referring to his painting.

'Yeah! Fucking great! Tell you what, though, it'll be good to get outta here for a few days, eh? Fuckin' women!'

'Er, you want to elaborate on that at all?' I asked, a little thrown by this tangential turn in the conversation.

'They're mad, Ben! I was talking to a woman last night, right, and we were doing old relationships 'n' stuff, yeah?'

'Right ...'

'Well, can you fuckin' believe it? I started telling her about some girlfriend I had about twenty years ago, who I got pretty attached to, right? Suddenly her mood changed! She started firing loadsa bloody personal questions at me about this woman from years ago. And from the tone of her voice and things, I could tell she was actually getting jealous! Jealous, Ben, of someone from fuckin' twenty years ago!

'They're all mad, Ben, they're all fuckin' mad!'

He was smiling by now, but the incident had obviously bewildered him.

'Anyway, Ben, here's to tomorrow, eh? Gotta get on with some painting. Have a good 'un!' And with that, he ambled out into the sun-dappled square, muttering as he strolled off down the narrow street towards his studio, '... mad ... all fuckin' mad ...'

I laughed, finished my coffee and headed for home in high spirits.

I would not have dreamt it possible that within twenty-four hours my world was to implode in the most dreadful manner imaginable.

The rest of Friday was occupied with my coming to grips with the task of frame assembly of monumental proportions. I checked the weather forecast for Saturday, and since there was no risk of rain overnight, the pieces were left in position on the terrace for final bolting together before Eric and I departed for England.

Saturday morning. I was happier than I had been for a very long time. Albeit difficult on a business level, the house was nonetheless completed, we were surrounded by a real community of caring people, we had a beautiful young family in good health, and the sun was, *comme d'habitude*, casting its consoling rays across the sadnesses of the recent past. And now, having by an amazing coincidence met another soulmate in the form of my dear friend Eric, I felt deeply optimistic about the exciting new challenge before us. I stood in the mottled morning light, screw gun in hand, contemplating the half-assembled framework at my feet, existing in the present and savouring one of life's exceptional moments.

I must have been in some sort of dreamlike state: I did not register the figure plunging down the steps towards the house until he was almost upon me.

Thierry. Arms flailing, sobbing uncontrollably. Standing, shaking, saying something. Something my brain understood but refused to acknowledge. His arms around me, his wet face against mine.

'*E ... E ... Eric ... oh, Ben ... Eric est m ... mort ...*'

Numb paralysis.

And now I'm turning away, face in hands, waiting for the horrorshock to disappear so I can continue with the frame.

Frame?

Frame?!

Chapter 40

My tears shape the perceived world into a gigantic hourglass, and me within, swirling around and around and down and down with the sands of tragic destiny, weightlessly being drawn into the abyss.

It's all going.

It's all gone.

Again.

Now I'm running down a road in a denied universe. Arriving at his place. Toy police in the fairy-tale reality stand guard around his window. Walking to the door, glimpse the cold body kneeling on a bed, head on hands on windowsill, contemplating sky.

Bruce, Arna, Thierry. Shared love. Shared tragedy.

Shared disbelieving silence.

Chapter 41

Eric had probably done more in sixty years than most people do in ninety. There was speculation as to the cause of death, but the peaceful expression upon the beautiful face at least helped us to believe that the end had been painless. Heart failure was diagnosed, possibly having been caused by an asthma attack just moments before; an inhaler had been found lying beside him at the open window. He had come to the mountains to breathe more freely, and had, it seemed, flung the windows wide to gaze upon the glory of the stars that night.

He had been married three times, and it was quite a crowd that gathered in the small village for the funeral preparations. We had the pleasure of accommodating Björk and Eric's youngest son, Thor, in one of the apartments below the house, and were also visited by some of the other members of Eric's large and diverse family. I had, of course, been eagerly looking forward to meeting young Beau again for some time, although I couldn't possibly have imagined that it would be under quite such surreal circumstances.

Friends and family came from far and wide to mourn the passing of their lost loved one. Preceding an open-air service in a village meadow, the closest family members held a private, agnostic remembrance in the medieval chapel set amongst the ruins overlooking the village, and later all retired to the village centre, where Thierry and Lyn opened their restaurant to the public. They had arranged a wonderful celebration of Eric's life based around several boxes of Newcastle Brown Ale, sent by a British well-wisher. Claudine allowed her bar to be used for the looped showing of the video Eric had made with Dave Stewart during the eighties.

The throng drank and made merry as the man would have wished; numerous and varied were the stories shared that day.

Dave Stewart himself returned to the region, playing a spontaneous rendition of Bob Dylan's *Knocking on Heaven's Door* in a small restaurant at Les Adrets that very same evening, and thus the man with whom I and countless others had shared so many precious moments finally passed out of our lives forever.

Chapter 42

Two days later, an abandoned, chocolate-coloured dog with a twinkle in its eye wandered into the village and followed us home. He has been with us ever since.

We named him Eric.

Acknowledgements

Capra, Fritjof; *The Tao of Physics*, Harper Collins UK; Shambhalla USA

Nicholas Treadwell – The Treadwell Gallery

The Eagle and The Hawk
Words by John Denver
Music by John Denver and Mike Taylor
Copyright © 1971; renewed 1999 Cherry Lane Music Publishing Company, Inc. (ASCAP), Dimensional.
Music of 1091 (ASCAP), Anna Kate Deutschendorf, Zachary Deutschendorf and Jesse Belle Denver
All Rights for Dimensional Music of 1091, Anna Kate Deutschendorf, Zachary Deutschendorf.
Administered by Cherry Lane Music Publishing Company inc.
All Rights for Jesse Belle Denver Administered by WB Music Corp.
International Copyright Secured All rights reserved.

Imagine
Words and Music by John Lennon © Copyright 1971 Lenono Music
Used by permission of Music Sales Limited.
All rights reserved, International Copyright Secured.

Money
Words and Music by Roger Waters © Roger Waters Music Overseas Ltd.
All rights administered by Warner/Chappell Music Ltd London W6 8BS
Reproduced by permission.

This is The Sea
Words and Music by Michael Scott © Dizzy Heights Music Publishing Ltd.
All rights administered by Warner/Chappell Music Ltd London W6 8BS
Reproduced by permission.

Pierre and Monique, without whom it may never have been possible.

Gréolières, late November.

Phillipe, pizza maestro, at 'La Barricade'.

The enormously charitable Claudine at 'La Vieille Auberge'.

Friends in need – Lyn and Thierry.

Hard times.

Paul was a breath of fresh air ...

Jean-Luc and Big Phil in jovial mood.

Gréolières, June.

Final touches.

... as if it had always been there.

Eric Scott, left, with the author and the finished portrait of Keith Richards.